A WATER LILY

AMONG THE WILDFLOWERS

Praise for
A Water Lily among the Wildflowers

"*A Water Lily among the Wildflowers* is a true account of what losing a child too soon looks like. Rachel's honest reflections about her experience with a second-trimester miscarriage points to the hope and healing that can be found after such a devastating loss. Her story will resonate with anyone navigating the tumultuous waters following one of life's most common and painful experiences that is rarely discussed. If you or someone you know has experienced the pain associated with pregnancy loss, this book is for you."

—**Elizabeth Gentry,** director of client services at Life Choices Rowan, author of *Return to Me*

"Rachel has given a gift to anyone who has been devastated by pregnancy loss. Her practical, perspective-shifting advice will help you move forward when you feel like you can't or shouldn't move on. She gently counsels you on how to handle unpredictable emotions and well-meaning but painful remarks by others. Most importantly, she offers hope."

—**Tanya Pollard,** Bible teacher, speaker, and author of *Memory Stones*

"Both vulnerable and insightful, this book sheds light on personal loss, but others can use it for general gain. There is a message throughout that shakes the hand of grief, benefitting from its work, but also, trusting in the hope that one day, grief will retire."

—**Megan Hood,** certified mental health coach, family advocate

"*A Water Lily among the Wildflowers* simply put is essential for anyone—woman or man—going through the devastation of losing a baby. Grief is never easy, but with this guide and the resources it includes, one can find the help, information, and encouragement to take the necessary steps to not just survive, but thrive after traumatic loss."

—**Leah Burris,** Christian mom of two earthly children and three babies in heaven, Labor and Delivery RN

A *Water Lily* among the Wildflowers

HOPE AND TRUTH FOR MOMS
AFTER PREGNANCY LOSS

Rachel Dickey

LEAFWOOD
PUBLISHERS
an imprint of Abilene Christian University Press

A WATER LILY AMONG THE WILDFLOWERS
Hope and Truth for Moms after Pregnancy Loss

Copyright © 2025 by Rachel Dickey

ISBN 978-1-68426-074-4

Printed in the United States of America

ALL RIGHTS RESERVED
No part of this publication may be reproduced, stored in a retrieval system, or transmitted in any form by any means—electronic, mechanical, photocopying, recording, or otherwise—without prior written consent.

Scripture quotations, unless otherwise noted, are from the Holy Bible, New International Version®, NIV®. Copyright © 1973, 1978, 1984, 2011 by Biblica, Inc.™ Used by permission of Zondervan. All rights reserved worldwide.

Scripture quotations are from the ESV® Bible (The Holy Bible, English Standard Version®), copyright © 2001 by Crossway, a publishing ministry of Good News Publishers. Used by permission. All rights reserved.

Scripture quotations noted NASB are taken from the New American Standard Bible® Copyright © 1960, 1962, 1963, 1968, 1971, 1972, 1973, 1975, 1977, 1995 by The Lockman Foundation. Used by permission.

Library of Congress Cataloging-in-Publication Data

Names: Dickey, Rachel, author.
Title: A waterlily among the wildflowers : hope and truth for moms after pregnancy loss / Rachel Dickey.
Description: Abilene, Texas: Leafwood Publishers, [2025] | Includes bibliographical references and index.
Identifiers: LCCN 2024021218 | ISBN 9781684260744 | ISBN 9781684268542 (ebook)
Subjects: LCSH: Fetal death—Religious aspects—Christianity. | Bereavement—Religious aspects—Christianity. | Mothers—Prayers and devotions.
Classification: LCC BV4907 .D53 2025 | DDC 248.8/66—dc23/eng/20240930
LC record available at https://lccn.loc.gov/2024021218

Cover design by Greg Jackson, Thinkpen Design
Interior text design by Scribe Inc.

Leafwood Publishers is an imprint of Abilene Christian University Press
ACU Box 29138
Abilene, Texas 79699
1-877-816-4455
www.leafwoodpublishers.com

25 26 27 28 29 30 31 / 7 6 5 4 3 2

*Dedicated to my God and Savior, Jesus Christ.
In the hardest days of my life
You showed yourself to me in ways I could
have never dreamed, and stretched me
farther than I could have ever imagined.
Thank you.*

*And to my son, Asher James.
Your life here,
though far shorter than I ever wanted,
changed me forever.*

Contents

Introduction	9
Chapter One: Lost	13
Chapter Two: Good Grief	25
Chapter Three: Bruises	45
Chapter Four: Till Death Do Us Part	63
Chapter Five: Certainty	83
Chapter Six: Anguish	109
Chapter Seven: Graves into Gardens	127
Bonus Chapter: For Dads *Written by Austin Dickey*	141
Acknowledgments	153
References	156
Gift Guide	157

Introduction

July 16, 2018

It was a special day.

My husband and I had just dropped off our two boys with my father-in-law and were on our way to our scheduled eighteen-week ultrasound to find out the gender (that we had been very eagerly waiting for) of our third baby. Although I have loved every second of it, boys had completely outnumbered girls in our house for more than four years. Trucks, tractors, dinosaurs, superheroes, and a lot of dirt had taken over my life. And I wondered if this baby might change things up a little bit. At this point, our dog and I had been the only girls in the house, and I think even she was hoping to have a little estrogen added to the mix, possibly meaning fewer wrestling matches for her, from at least one of the kiddos.

When we asked our boys whether they thought their new sibling would be a boy or girl, they were at first very certain they were getting a sister, but as the weeks went by, they insisted that this baby had to be a boy. Not a single one of us truly cared what gender the baby would be, but by then, all of us had been anticipating the news for a very long time.

As we drove to the appointment together, I looked out the window, daydreaming about the newest member of our family, who we were about to get to know a little bit better. I kept picturing all the different scenarios of what life was going to be like as we became a family of five. How much fun life with three boys would be, and that I should probably start a separate bank account just for food and emergency room bills. Or possibly, how I should be preparing myself for the amount of pink that could consume our house if we had a girl and face the fact that I was going to have to comb at least one of my children's hair every day.

My daydreaming was interrupted as we pulled up to the OB-GYN office. This was the same office I had been to for the last four years. The same one that cared and provided for me during my last two pregnancies, and the same one where we learned the gender of our other babies. It had become a special place for us. Our conversations with the staff had become more than just the usual check-in mantra. They knew each of us by name and asked about specific details of each of our lives.

As we sat in the waiting room that day, I took in each of the women I saw. Some were there by themselves, and I wondered if this was their first pregnancy or if they had other children elsewhere. Others were there with their families, and I saw the challenge of trying to keep little ones entertained in a quiet waiting room—a challenge I was very familiar with. But it also reminded me that soon I would be balancing three, and waiting rooms were going to once again look very different.

As they called our name, I felt my stomach flip around with a combination of both nervousness and excitement. The nurse directed us to the ultrasound technician and jokingly walked us through what was about to happen as if we had never done this before. We both laughed and followed instructions. We explained that we had a gender reveal party scheduled in a few days and would like for her to write "Boy" or "Girl" on a piece of paper and put it in an envelope for us so that we could find out together later.

Austin and I have always discovered the gender together first, before having friends and family over and revealing it to them in some sort of fun way. It has always been a special moment for just the two of us. A moment to celebrate, cry happy tears, anticipate what is to come, and most importantly, start praying for our future son or daughter.

I lay down on the table, just as I had many times before. As the technician directed Austin on where to sit, I smiled at him and jokingly said, "Are you ready?" She reminded us that nothing would appear on the TV screen at first, just so that we wouldn't accidentally see "something" that might give it away; for the next couple of minutes, we sat together in silence.

There was nothing in those minutes that could have prepared us for what was about to come.

CHAPTER ONE

Lost

July 16, 2018

I looked around the room as the technician began our eighteen-week scan, noticing how perfect it was for viewing ultrasounds. There were no windows, and it was completely dark except for a lamp on the desk in the corner. A chair for dads was next to the table I was lying on, facing the TV hung on the wall. It was a perfect setup for parents anxiously waiting to see their babies. As I lay on that table taking in all the details of that room, I remember thinking to myself, "Normally we can at least hear the heartbeat, just not see anything on the screen." I thought to myself, "Maybe the sound is just muted." I almost asked the technician if she could turn the sound on so we could just sit and listen to the heartbeat, but I held off, thinking she was probably just very focused and would turn the sound on in a few minutes.

She kept looking at the screen, not saying a word. Every once in a while, I would hear a few clicks. It seemed to me as if she was just analyzing everything, taking measurements, checking all the organs, and possibly struggling to determine what gender this baby was. She hid her fear very well. About three minutes of complete silence went by, and then she said the words that still paralyze me today:

"I'm sorry, I don't know any other way of saying this. There's no heartbeat."

I stared straight at the wall in front of me. It was a dull gray/beige color, with no patterns or designs. Its simplicity was helpful because it allowed me to try to actually process what was just said, and that this was actually happening. I kept staring at one single spot on that blank wall; it was like my mind knew it couldn't take in anything else—that if I turned my eyes anywhere else in the room and tried to process something other than what was just said, my brain would explode.

What felt like hours but was only a matter of seconds went by, and then the technician said, "I'm going to go grab the doctor. I'll be right back."

I immediately grabbed Austin's hand and squeezed harder than I ever had. His chair was positioned behind me, so we couldn't see one another's faces, but we didn't need to. The terror in that room was so thick, nothing could have made its way through.

Neither one of us said a word. We were paralyzed with fear. I felt like I couldn't even take a full breath, because if I did, my body would shatter into a million pieces. Nausea crept in slowly, and every few seconds, I began to shake uncontrollably from head to toe.

I begged God to let our doctor be there that day. He had been through everything with us. I had seen him for all my *other appointments, he delivered our other two boys, and he had graciously once again agreed to deliver this one.*

It was, in fact, his day to be at the hospital and not at the office. Thankfully, one of the nurses I used to work with (who was now a nurse practitioner) came running in. Somehow, seeing someone I recognized and knew made this seem a little less real and, if only for a second, less likely to be true.

She checked over everything just like the technician had done, and for a few seconds, we both had an ounce of hope that she would find the heartbeat. That somehow the technician had missed it, or that it just miraculously started beating again. She turned to us and in the most heartbroken way said, "I'm sorry."

She didn't need to say any more. Those two words made it very clear. Two professionally trained people had searched all they could to find that heartbeat. They wanted that heart to beat as badly as we did. But in that room, on that particular day, the heartbeat was gone, and so was our son, Asher.

* * *

The beginning of every human life is sacred. It's something that our minuscule minds cannot fully comprehend; the complexity of how each individual part, down to the smallest microscopic cell, perfectly knit together to form one body working in complete harmony is something that is beyond anything our minds will ever truly understand. Yes, science and technology have absolutely given us an incredible, in-depth understanding of it and even some very powerful photos, but God is the only one who fully understands the entire creation of each and every person.

One thing, however, that is most certainly understood by every individual is that one day, each person's life will end. Each of us knows that death is inevitable. Not a single person is exempt from it. We might not know the day, the time, or possibly even the way, but we do know that at some point, our lives and the lives of the people we love will end.

For some, though, death seems to come too soon, and it's hard not to question why some people get to live longer than others. It's hard not to put "deservedness" on who should live and who shouldn't. Why does a serial killer get to live but a two-year-old has to die from starvation or child abuse? Why does a college graduate have to get hit walking down the street by a drunk driver or a thirty-eight-year-old firefighter with four children have to die in an arsonous fire saving other people's lives?

And for a mother who has lost a baby, this "death that comes too soon" resonates deeply. We try to make sense of what doesn't seem fair or even logical. And it seems impossible to wrap our brains around the fact that our precious babies only got to live a few weeks or months, and a million questions begin to overwhelm our minds.

There is something we've never felt before deep within us that cries out to God, pleading with him that this cannot possibly be his plan. An agony we've never felt before unfolds, and a wrestling with God that we never anticipated our lives would hold begins.

> "Why would you even allow me to get pregnant
> if you were just going to take him away?"
>
> "Why didn't you protect him?"

"Father, please bring him back."

"Why eighteen weeks?"

"Why me?"

I knew God was good, but this was not. I knew that death was never in his original plan, yet the reality of it was here, and it had not just gently knocked on our door; it had violently kicked it down and stormed its way in. I asked over and over, "Why, God? I don't understand why you would take him away already," yet the only answer that seemed to echo back was silence.

And in that silence, I came up with a million different possibilities to try to give myself something to cling to. But all that did was make denial sink in further. All my brain could run through were a million "what ifs" and "if onlys."

"*What if* they missed something on the monitor? Maybe he has a heart condition, and when we go back they will be able to find the heartbeat again. I've heard countless stories of people's hearts stopping and then starting again. Jesus is God Almighty and has raised people from the dead; I absolutely believe he could make his heart start beating again."

Or, *if only* he had made it a few more weeks, and then maybe we found out there was a problem; he could have possibly been delivered early, placed in the NICU, and had a chance to survive.

Denial planted itself deep into my bones, and I kept trying to come up with a reason for my baby to still be alive and be here, even though deep down I knew he was gone.

And then those "what ifs" and "if onlys" shifted into "Was this my fault? Was there something I did to cause this? Could I have prevented this?" One by one, my thoughts would continually spiral out of control.

> "I ate my steak medium-rare instead of well-done."
> "I had too much stress."
> "I didn't put gloves on one time when I was cleaning."
> "I worked out too hard or lifted too heavy of a box."

As mothers, we have an innate drive to protect our children. Babies are innocent and need protecting, so it would of course be normal for us to be designed to do anything in our power to protect them. And we feel a tremendous amount of guilt when we aren't able to achieve that. We think to ourselves, "It had to have happened because of me. I was the one carrying him. I was the one who controlled what my body did and what went inside of it. It was my job to protect him, and I didn't." Those feelings completely overwhelm our minds, and it feels impossible to shake them.

With Asher, we were incredibly grateful to be able to see after I delivered him what likely caused his death. We saw that the end of the umbilical cord that was attached to him (where his belly button would have been) was much smaller and narrower than the rest of the cord, and as we looked over the cord, we could see a blood clot about halfway down. It was evident that that blood clot and abnormally narrow cord were what caused his death.

Yet even knowing the cause, I still had moments where I believed that I had to have done something that led to his death. I had nights where I had complete breakdowns, almost to the point of hyperventilating, truly believing that it was somehow my fault.

And for many women, the exact cause of their baby's death is not known and will never be known. So many mothers will come up with a reason or a cause for it, to help fill that unbearable void that's there now. Understandably, it seems impossible and unfair to accept the fact that the exact cause of our baby's death will never be known. Our brains turn that into "There was no reason for them to die." Yet they did die, and so we have a deep desire to validate it.

A deep desire to be able to rationalize it some way, somehow. To give meaning to their life, because so much of the world tells us there isn't any meaning to it. So much of the world says they weren't real, they didn't "exist," they weren't alive, or they weren't even a child. Yet nothing could be further from the truth.

* * *

The title of this book, *A Water Lily among the Wildflowers*, was inspired by a beautiful painting gifted to me by a friend after we lost Asher. The painting consisted of three flowers, each representing one of my boys. At the time, I did not know that each month also has a birth flower just like each month has a birthstone.

On this painting was a paperwhite narcissus for the month of December (for my eldest), a daffodil for the month of March (for my middle son), and a water lily for the month of July (for Asher). As I admired the painting and saw the water lily, I was immediately intrigued and began researching all about them.

What I learned is that there are over seventy varieties of water lilies, each being unique in shape, size, color, fragrance, and blooming pattern, and they are found in lakes and ponds all over the world. But what I also discovered is that the life cycle of a water lily is very different from that of any other kind of flower.

They begin their lives by sprouting from the muck and mud at the bottom of a pond or lake, and the majority of their lives are then spent growing underwater, completely unseen. When they finally emerge above the surface and then bloom, the actual flower blossom only lasts for three or four days before it dies and returns back to the bottom of the water. Its life and beauty are very short-lived.

I then thought about water lilies compared to the rest of the flowers of the world. Specifically, I pictured a vast field full of wildflowers. I thought about how each of those individual flowers in that field is distinct and unique in its own way (just as water lilies are), but that each flower grows and lives the typical life cycle of a flower, and there, a beautiful connection was made.

Our babies are the water lilies in a world full of wildflowers.

Just like water lilies, these beautiful babies spend their lives growing completely unseen from the world and only live for a short amount of time before they die. Yet that short amount of time they are with us, that short amount of time they "bloom," doesn't take away by any means from their beauty or how much they are cherished.

They are here, though we do not get to have them for very long. They are uniquely and perfectly designed and created, they are loved, and they are cherished. But their lives look so different, and they are much shorter than we ever imagined they would be.

In a single fleeting moment, they are gone, and along with them, all our hopes and dreams for that beautiful person that was created inside each of us begin to melt away. All the joys that come with being a parent, everything we've looked forward to slowly dissipates, and we grieve what would have been.

We grieve the excitement of learning who God created them to be and discovering a little more of their personalities each year, observing what their challenges in life might be versus what comes easily to them, watching their little bodies grow and change, developing from one stage to the next.

We grieve the simple and still moments of taking them in with each of our senses. Feeling their tiny hands wrap around our fingers. Seeing them smile for the first time or hearing the sound of their voices as they say their first word; the euphoria that stirs in us as we listen to them belly laugh. Or watching peace pour over them as they melt into our chests when we rock them to sleep, all because they know they are safe in our arms.

We grieve watching them take their first steps and their need to hold on to us as they learn to walk so they don't fall. Watching their faces light up as they learn something new about the world around them. Late nights at the ball field and rehearsals before the big shows.

Each and every birthday.

We grieve the moments they cling to us when they are scared or hurt, knowing that one day they won't need us anymore. The driving lessons in the parking lot down the road and picking out what to wear for their first dates. Dropping them off for their first job interviews and the bittersweet excitement as they open the response letters from college applications.

Every moment is now only a picture of what would have been—of what *should* have been but can no longer be. We know this and understand this, but we don't know where to go from here. How do we move forward? How do we heal?

We do it with help.

Help from our heavenly Father and help from others.

Our God is not a distant God sitting on a throne up above, watching as we scramble through life, waiting to see if we "figure it out" on our own. He is a God who loves us and cares for us deeply, a God who lifts us up and carries us through our hurts, and a God who wants nothing more than to have a true relationship with us and to heal us in the way that only he can. Hagar gave God the name El Roi, "the God who sees me" (Gen. 16:13), and it is absolutely true for you too. He sees you and knows your hurt and offers every part of himself to help carry you.

Additionally, our help comes from one another. God created us not only to be in community with him but also to be in community with one another (1 Cor. 12:25–27; Matt. 18:20). He never intended for us to walk through this life alone. In Scripture, God shows us that even *before* the creation of the world, he himself was not alone. He was in community with Jesus and the Holy Spirit (Gen. 1:2, 1:26; John 1:1), and he created a world that mirrored that—a world that was designed for people to be together.

I know that in the midst of grief, it can be hard to allow other people to come into our lives. Our minds are so clouded, it makes it hard to think, and it's hard to trust people when we're in those vulnerable places. I promise you, though, it's worth it.

In the moments when I've chosen to share the news of Asher's death with others (especially in the weeks immediately following his death), multiple people shared the stories of the losses they'd experienced, and it gave me so much comfort knowing I wasn't alone. It was so encouraging to know that someone had walked through what I'd walked through, to know they'd truly experienced the same hurt and pain, and to validate some of the confusion I was feeling. And so many offered beautiful words of comfort that I would have otherwise missed out on.

God places people in our lives in the midst of our trials to help us. Maybe one person has gotten to the other side of whatever trial we are facing and can offer comfort or guidance as we walk through it. Or maybe that person is smack-dab in the middle of the same trial, and we now have a friend to walk side by side with as we get through it.

And sometimes people are placed in your life for the sole purpose of being a support for you. They haven't walked through the exact trial you are facing, but they offer ears to listen and shoulders to cry on. They offer to bring you food, clean your house, or watch your other children so you can have a moment to grieve. Most importantly, they make sure you know you are not alone.

I know how heavy your heart is. And I know how much you hurt, how much your entire body aches from this pain. I have felt it and walked through it. But I promise that it is possible to heal and be happy again. It is possible to lift your head off the pillow without feeling like it weighs a thousand pounds. It's possible to want to go and do things again without feeling guilty, and it's possible to hold another baby without crying.

As a friend and a woman who has walked through this, I will be right here with you, sharing with you all that I have learned—particularly what the Bible says about all that you are feeling. These chapters will unpack what Scripture says about unborn babies and their salvation, God's love for them, and grief and grieving and how that may look different between men and women. It will unpack what Scripture says about the sometimes well-intentioned but mostly hurtful statements others say regarding your baby and what it says about suffering, particularly suffering the loss of a child. God knew the millions of people who would walk through this trial, and he graciously provided Scripture to help with our hardest and most difficult questions.

Know that he is a God who understands grief, a God who has suffered and who *willingly* experienced the loss of his own Son just so that this curse of death would not lead to eternal separation from him and who gave us the only Hope that carries us forward after the loss of our babies. He hurts and aches right alongside you throughout every step of this journey (2 Cor. 1:3–7), and he promises to be right next to you, continually holding you up.

CHAPTER TWO

Good Grief

July 25, 2018

It's raining today. It's been raining for a few days now, and I don't really mind it. It's peaceful, and it quiets my soul. How does rain do that? Something that can be very loud and invasive makes us stop, be still, and listen. I especially love the sound of it on our metal roof.

But today as I look and listen, there's a longing in my heart to be able to hold you again. Just one week ago, I was holding you. I was looking at you and studying you and admiring every part of you. I've sat multiple times in this house, holding and rocking each of your brothers, listening to the sound of the rain on our roof, but I'll never have the chance to do that with you.

I miss you.

I cannot wait to see you in heaven. What will you look like? Will you be a fully grown man? Will you stand taller than me? What color will your hair and eyes be? What will your voice sound like? What will you love to do?

> The ache is so deep today. I keep getting rumbles in my stomach in the same exact spot where you were just kicking me, and I keep thinking it's you. For that single fleeting moment, I forget that you're gone, and I still feel pregnant.
>
> I don't know where to go from here. Everything seems wrong to do.
>
> I want to pick up my book from my Bible study that I was just reading two weeks ago, and I want to keep reading and learning. I want to turn on a favorite movie or show or go out to eat at one of our usual restaurants; I want to do anything that we used to do when life was "normal," but it all seems so wrong.
>
> It feels like if I do anything the way it was before, it means that I'm forgetting you. I can't just pick up and go back to the way things were before this happened.
>
> I've heard over time things will get easier, but for now, everything just seems wrong.

Grief is one of the first things someone talks about after a death or traumatic event, yet I feel like it's one of the last things fully understood.

It's uniquely complex, and that makes it challenging to define.

Everyone seems to have a different definition for it, and I have learned that in a lot of ways, it does have to be defined subjectively. Each person's loss is uniquely personal, and their journey through grief will be unique as well. This means that no two mothers are going to grieve the loss of their babies the same.

But although grief is not identical for each person, there are often similarities. And when you are in the midst of it, it's incredibly relieving to know others experience some of the same things you have, and this helps you feel prepared to deal with challenging moments when they arise.

For example, some of the questions that ran through my head were

> "Do other moms get triggered at the sound of a newborn baby crying too?"
>
> "Is it normal for me to constantly feel like his death had to have been my fault somehow?"

The unfortunate truth is we live in a world where talking about miscarriage, stillbirth, and pregnancy loss just doesn't happen. The conversations have been quieted and pushed under the rug, making it hard for grieving mothers to know what to expect and/or not expect. And it's made it difficult for other people to know how to comfort grieving mothers, leaving many women feeling alone and isolated.

But part of what I discovered is that many women, though we all grieve differently, do experience a lot of the same feelings and emotions. And many of the same situations and scenarios that are hard for one woman are also hard for other women as well. The silver lining in that is it brings us all together, and we can lean on each other through our darkest moments.

This chapter is by no means an exhaustive guide to every component or aspect of the grieving process. I know for me, in my deepest days of grief, I could not have sat and read scientific and reference studies regarding grief or bereavement. My brain was just too tired and overwhelmed. But what brought me great comfort was learning bits and pieces of some of that information so I could know that what I was experiencing was something many other mothers had experienced as well. I could rest in knowing I wasn't alone and could have help navigating the depths of this overwhelming grief.

However, there are *tons* of wonderful resources such as books, pastors, counselors, and loss groups that can help you sort through the deepest parts of your grief and gather back up all the pieces of your shattered heart. And I would encourage you to reach out and ask, or begin researching yourself, if there are areas where you would like to know more or if you feel like your grief has gotten to a level where depression might be a factor. The references section in this book provides some links to find a Christian grief counselor near you.

As you maneuver through all that this grief holds and discover what is common for many mothers, some things may resonate with you, and some may not. That's OK. Some things that were true for me may not be for you, and vice versa. It's going to look different for everyone. And one of the most beautiful and comforting treasures we get to cling to is the fact that we have a Savior who fully understands our needs and meets us *exactly* where we are in our loss. He meets us in our confusion, he meets us in our anger, he meets us in our questioning, and he meets us in our sadness.

And then he abundantly gives us exactly what we need.

My hope is that no matter where you are in your journey, whether your son or daughter died yesterday or twenty years ago, you will know you are not alone, and you will understand a little more about what this particular grief can look like. The following are a few things I've come to understand about grief.

NO ONE WILL GRIEVE THE SAME AS ANYONE ELSE

There is no way of knowing or determining how a person will grieve. No matter what circumstance or what walk of life they are in, each and every person will grieve death differently. Yes, there will likely be some similarities in the way people grieve, but grief will never be identical for any two people.

And this is especially true for mothers who have lost a baby. Our situations are the same, but the circumstances surrounding those situations are different. For one mother, this might have been her first loss, and it may have been a loss following another traumatic event in her life, like the loss of one of her parents. For another mother, this might have been her third or fourth loss after countless months of trying to conceive a baby. Both women have experienced loss, but because of the circumstances surrounding those losses, their grief is going to look vastly different.

Therefore, there is not, nor will there ever be, a "right" way to grieve. There's no way to determine exactly what course grief will take, and there is no handbook to follow that will guide you to the end of it. For me, that is where we can take comfort. We can take the pressure off ourselves to act a certain way or meet a certain "standard" or "deadline" in healing. And most importantly, we can *give ourselves grace*.

I encourage you to try not to compare your loss to anyone else's. It can be easy to look at how one mom is walking through her grief and think you should be walking or feeling or doing the same as her. But that couldn't be further from the truth. Your loss is your own. Take each day, each feeling, and each circumstance one at a time.

EACH PERSON WILL GRIEVE EVERY DEATH THEY EXPERIENCE DIFFERENTLY

The loss of someone's father will be grieved differently than the loss of their mother, and the loss of someone's child will be grieved differently than the loss of their spouse. This is also true for mothers who have lost more than one baby. She will grieve each one of her babies individually. A mother's first loss will look very different from her second, third, and so on. This is necessary and beautiful because each baby that a woman loses is unique and individual. And a mother will grieve uniquely and individually for each child.

DIFFERENT PEOPLE WILL GRIEVE THE SAME DEATH DIFFERENTLY

Specifically, when it comes to the loss of our babies, each person will grieve that loss differently. Mothers, fathers, spouses, grandmas, grandpas, sisters, brothers, aunts, uncles, friends, and so on will all have their own ways of grieving. There is no right or wrong way, but each will look different from the other. Each person had, and would have had, different roles in our babies' lives; therefore, their grief will reflect the loss of their role. And sometimes the way that others grieve is hard for us to understand or accept. The next two chapters dive deeper into this.

THERE IS NO TIMELINE FOR GRIEF

Let's clarify that despite what much of the rest of the world tells you, there is no timeline to be met with grief. I've heard countless stories about how mothers were shamed for "still being upset" about their loss after an allotted time—a time that someone else had decided on. Or they were told that this is a loss that doesn't need to be grieved altogether.

There is no certain way that you should be acting or feeling by any decided time. There is no way to control grief or control when your emotions will cease being so raw. Yes, as time goes on, things will get easier, but there may also be days where emotions come flooding back, and you may not have any control over it. There will be certain circumstances that you weren't expecting to be hard that will be hard. And there will be stories and situations that will arise that could bring you to your knees.

Grief is something we will carry with us for the rest of our lives here on earth until we get to heaven. Photographer Noelle Mirabella shared on social media a conversation she had with one of her clients, Thelma, who was 102 years old. As she and Thelma chatted, she learned that Thelma lost her first daughter, Francis, at two months old. Noelle then, through her tears, shared that she lost her first daughter, Ava Marie, as well. As the two shared with each other about their babies that were no longer here, Noelle then said, "I just have one question for you. *Does it still hurt?*" Thelma was blind, so she did not look back at Noelle when she answered but instead "looked straight ahead and raised her chin a little bit, very strong and poised in her conviction," and answered, "*Yes, it still hurts.*"[1]

At 102 years old, it still hurts. Do not feel the need to rush your healing; be gentle with yourself, and know that the only time frame that is absolute will be heaven.

DAYS WHERE YOU FEEL LIKE YOU'VE TAKEN STEPS BACK IN YOUR GRIEF

I had multiple days where I could easily talk about my son without feeling a single tear come to my eyes, and then literally the next day, I would be talking to a different person, saying the exact same words I said the day before, and it would be as if someone turned on the water faucets. This was so frustrating at times and made me feel like I had taken steps back in my grief. It made me feel like I wasn't healing and must not have been doing something right. But the truth is, that is completely normal. That is grief.

I believe it's why so many people refer to it as a journey, because you are transitioning from one place to another, but you will have valleys to trudge through and mountains to climb. And there will be times when you will hit rough territory, or storms will come out of nowhere and make it that much harder. It doesn't mean that you are doing anything wrong; it's just part of the pilgrimage.

YOUR PHYSICAL BODY CAN CHANGE DRAMATICALLY

I saw a picture on social media a few months after I lost Asher that resonated with me in many ways. It was a sculpture of a person crouching on the ground made of four thousand pounds of rocks.[2] Though the artist didn't create it for the purpose of representing grief, thousands of people who viewed the image immediately associated it with what our bodies feel like when we are walking through grief—the heaviness of thousands of rocks weighing us down, making it feel impossible to even lift an arm, much less be able to stand. It was a beautiful representation of the physical effects that manifest within a body accompanied by grief because the list seems endless:

> Aches and pains, digestive issues, brain fog, headaches, trouble concentrating and paying attention, sleep issues, anxiety, panic attacks, depression, mood swings, chest pain, heart issues, shortness of breath, nausea, exhaustion, lowered immune systems, and even clumsiness.

In a study published by the National Library of Medicine, researchers concluded that "the loss of an infant through stillbirth, miscarriage, or neonatal death is recognized as a traumatic life event" and therefore can have the physical and emotional repercussions of any traumatic event.[3] And so, if your body seems to have ailments it's never had before, or if you're behaving differently than you ever have, know that it could absolutely be from the trauma of losing your baby.

TRIGGERS

Triggers are experiences, people, places, things, and so on that immediately remind you of your loss and can plunge you back into the deepest areas of your grief. Each woman may have triggers that are harder for her than others, or she may have many things that trigger her while some women may only have a few.

Here are some common triggers for this specific type of grief:

- hearing and/or seeing a newborn baby
- seeing another pregnant woman
- seeing people or places that remind you of your baby
- hearing and/or seeing pregnancy or birth announcements
- experiencing holidays (knowing that your family doesn't feel complete)
- going to events and celebrations specifically surrounding babies (baby showers, gender reveals, etc.)
- hearing or reading about other moms' losses
- watching TV shows or movies where loss happens

For someone who has never experienced the loss of a baby, it's hard to know how to navigate through these when they happen. I know at some point in my journey, I have experienced each one of these. Many of them more than once. They can be challenging and painful, but there are things that can help you get through them.

PLANNING FOR AND COPING WITH TRIGGERS

There will be situations where you will be aware ahead of time of things that may trigger you. This might include being invited to an event where you know one of the women who will be there is pregnant, or looking at your calendar and seeing the baby shower you RSVP'd for before you lost your baby. These are examples of instances you can plan for, and you can decide ahead of time how you will handle them, knowing you may be triggered.

But there will also be some triggers that you won't be able to plan for. They will be subtle or abrupt things that hit you out of nowhere. An unexpected pregnancy announcement, a song that brings you to your knees, a scene in a TV show or commercial, something on social media, a pregnant woman in a store, a place where you're reminded you will never be able to take your baby, and so on. Unfortunately, those are going to come up. But here are a few ways you can respond when expected or unexpected triggers arise:

- You can allow yourself to grieve in that moment if you feel safe.
- You can choose to avoid that situation.
- You can keep yourself distracted.

Any of these responses are OK. If there is a situation where you don't feel emotionally safe enough to grieve, then it's absolutely OK to walk away and avoid that situation entirely. Or, if you are comfortable and are with people who will support you in your grief (as opposed to shaming you), then absolutely take that moment to grieve.

Something that eased my soul was making a plan for how I would handle unexpected triggers when they occurred. Creating a strategy for what to do with those feelings and triggers can keep you from avoiding going anywhere at all. It lets your brain and body know it's safe to do this.

Devise a plan for what you will do if there is a newborn crying in the grocery store. Maybe it's moving yourself to the other side of the store where you can't hear the baby anymore. Or maybe it's going to sit in your car for a few minutes, allowing yourself to grieve as much as you need. Or maybe there is a Scripture verse that is very comforting that you can write down and carry with you. Anytime you need, pull that verse out, and repeat it over yourself. Eventually, you will memorize it.

One of my favorites was Psalm 73:26: "My flesh and my heart may fail, but God is the strength of my heart and my portion forever."

I would repeat "He is the strength of my heart. He is the strength of my heart" over and over, and it would calm me.

The triggers that you know are coming—like a baby shower, upcoming holidays, or the due date of a friend having a baby—are a little easier to plan for. When you are ready, look at your calendar, make yourself aware of future events, and decide how you want to approach them. The first year after losing a loved one is nicknamed the "Year of Firsts." These are holidays, anniversaries, and experiences that you will have to go through for the first time without the person you've lost—the first Christmas, the first birthday without them, the first anniversary of their death, the first time you hold a baby after losing yours, and so on. And they are considered significant milestones in someone's grief. Those days are inevitably going to be hard, but the good thing is that you know they are coming, and you can prepare for them.

Some women choose to avoid the day completely, keeping themselves distracted with other things so they can get through the day. Others make sure they are in a safe environment, either by themselves or with people who will support them in their grief, and they take the day as it comes. Neither way is right or wrong.

The important thing to remember is that your feelings and your reactions to something that is triggering for you are not bad. Remember that even though triggers are painful, they do not mean that you are failing to heal or move forward. Your brain is doing exactly what it was designed to do. It is reminding you of something similar that caused fear or pain before in order to protect you from it happening again. Instead of being afraid of triggers, allow them to be moments to lean into your Father and opportunities to begin healing.

* * *

> Thank you for giving us a way to express our deepest emotions. I don't know what I would do if I couldn't release the pain in my heart.
> —Jill Kelly, *Prayers of Hope for the Brokenhearted*

The Bible is not silent on grief.

It is not quiet on the weeping and mourning the people of God expressed because of love and pain. And I think it's crucial as believers to fully comprehend that we have a God who loves us so deeply that he conveyed in the Word that grieving is something we can embrace and understand as part of our journey.

Let's look a little closer at some of what Scripture tells us about grief/grieving.

DO NOT BE AFRAID OR ASHAMED TO GRIEVE

God created our emotions. He made us emotional beings in his image; therefore, it is in no way sinful or wrong to show those emotions. And there is no reaction or response that surprises God or that he cannot handle. Displaying emotions such as grief also does not indicate a lack of faith, but rather it reveals honest sorrow at the reality of suffering and death.

We see this in Scripture in something called laments. Laments within the Bible are prayers, conversations, vents, and poems from God's people expressing sorrow, pain, or confusion to God, and there are lots of them.

The book of Habakkuk, for example, has many poems of lament, where the prophet Habakkuk shares his personal struggle to believe that God is good when there is so much tragedy and evil in the world. And over one-third of all the Psalms are laments, including both individual and community ones (Pss. 10, 12–14, and many others).

Lament is also displayed often in the book of Job. Job did not try to hide his overwhelming grief and the questions he had for the Lord. In fact, he did the opposite. He "tore his robe, shaved his head and fell to the ground in worship," questioned

God, and even cursed the day he was born (Job 1:20–22). Yet Scripture tells us that even in all of that, he did not sin, and he did not lose his faith in God (1:22).

Second Samuel 1:11–12 shows us that David and his men did something similar to grieve the loss of King Saul and their friend Jonathan, and in Genesis 50:1–11, we are told Joseph mourned and grieved over the loss of his father, Jacob, for many months.

God also gifted us with an entire book of lament, called Lamentations (I talk more about this in Chapter Seven), made up of five poems, each expressing different facets of grief people experienced after the destruction of Jerusalem.

Our Father purposefully put multiple accounts in Scripture that included the expression of grief for us to understand that we do not have to suffer in silence. God does not ask his people to deny their emotions but to voice their feelings and pour them out before the Lord. Do not be afraid or ashamed to grieve the loss of your baby. In today's world, that is hard to do because we have so many other voices telling us to sweep our grief under the rug and pretend like it didn't happen. But Solomon tells us in Ecclesiastes 3:4 there is "a time to weep" and "a time to mourn" just as there is "a time to laugh" and "a time to dance." Scripture shows us it is OK to give your heart permission to grieve the loss of your baby no matter what anyone else says to you.

Grief was designed by our perfect Creator as a means to express our deepest pain over the things we love the most. God has purposefully woven into Scripture the words of grief addressed to him so that we may know he welcomes us to bring all our emotions and lay them at his feet.

OUR SAVIOR KNOWS WHAT IT IS TO GRIEVE

The books of Matthew and Mark tell us that right before Jesus is handed over to be crucified, he retreats to pray in the garden of Gethsemane and says, "My soul is deeply grieved to the point of death" (Matt. 26:38; Mark 14:34 NASB). Jesus experienced crushing grief that felt impossible to survive. He knew what had to be done but still asked God to take away what he was calling him to walk through. He knows what it means to sorrow to the point that you think you can't live through it or that you just simply don't want to live through it.

I remember the mornings when I opened my eyes from sleeping and was immediately plunged back into the reality that Asher was gone and that this was still happening. My body felt like it weighed a thousand pounds, and I could barely lift my head. I didn't want to get up. I didn't want to try to move forward with all that God was still calling me to do. I had a husband, two young boys, a house, and responsibilities. But there was a part of me that just didn't want to do all that life encompassed anymore. And there were moments when I felt like there was no way I would survive the journey through all this.

Rest in knowing your Savior has felt that weight (and much more). The prophet Isaiah declared years beforehand that the Messiah to come would be a "man of sorrows and acquainted with grief" (Isa. 53:3). And Jesus modeled for us while he was here on earth what to do when we experience that grief too. He showed us three things.

He Weeps

The eleventh chapter of John is the account of the death and resurrection of Lazarus. The purpose of the account of Lazarus's death was to show Jesus's power over death. Jesus purposefully waited before he answered Mary and Martha's call when Lazarus was ill, and he purposefully waited until after Lazarus had been dead for days to convey to the world that he not only had the power to stop death from happening (as Martha said to him in verse 21) but that he was also the resurrection and the life and had complete power over death.

But when Jesus came to Mary and Martha, he found them weeping over their brother's death, and "Jesus wept" with them (John 11:35).

This expression of emotion by Jesus strikes me every time I read it. I can't imagine what it must have been like to witness the God of the universe weeping. Jesus being both God and man, both divine and human, and the complete image of God the Father communicates to us here how God relates and connects to the world through emotion. It communicates to us that God the Father and the Son weep with those who weep and sorrow over death.

And what resonates so deeply with this particular account where we see Jesus weep is that Jesus foreknew that he would raise Lazarus from the dead. He knew it was not the end of Lazarus's life on earth.

He foretold in verse 4 before Lazarus died that "this illness does not lead to death. It is for the glory of God so that the Son of God may be glorified through it." Yet we see him pause and weep despite knowing. Jesus had compassion and empathy for Mary and Martha and felt and expressed sorrow about his friend's death. And verse 33 says that when he saw Mary and the other Jews weeping, "he was deeply moved in his spirit and greatly troubled." Jesus outwardly expressed the love in his heart. Verse 36 confirms this when the Jews who witnessed his weeping said, "See how he loved him!"

All the while, knowing that Lazarus's life on earth was to be restored.

In this chapter, Jesus conveyed to us that crying is in no way wrong. It does not mean you are weak, as much of the world tells us, and it does not mean you lack faith. It is an expression of the heart, and the God of the universe humbled himself to show us that. He showed us that it is OK to weep for those you love: "You have kept count of my tossings; put my tears in your bottle. Are they not in your book?" (Ps. 56:8 ESV).

How comforting is this image of God catching our tears and keeping account of them? He sees our grief, and just as Jesus entered into the grief of the mourners of Lazarus, God enters our grief as well.

He Retreats to a Quiet Place to Pray

The previous portions of Scripture we examined in Matthew and Mark, where Jesus is grieved to the point of death, show us that in his deepest distress, Jesus goes to a quiet place away from everyone else to cry out to his Father. He shows us that in our darkest hours of need, the place we need to go to, the person we need to talk with, is our Father. There is no one else, nor any location, nor any other distraction that can do that for us. There's no amount of TV shows we could binge-watch, no beach vacation that's long enough, and no person (not even the person who loves us the most and knows us the best) that will be able to sustain us the way that the Father does. He is the one who will carry us and fill us with living water in our heavy grieving moments.

He Uses His Grief to Further the Kingdom

In Matthew 14:13-14, after Jesus hears of John the Baptist's death, he is deeply grieved and gets on a boat to go to a desolate place. But before he reaches the other shore, he sees there is a crowd of people there waiting for him. I can imagine all he wanted to do in that moment was grieve the loss of his close relative and friend, yet there were people waiting for him, demanding his attention, and needing healing from him. Scripture tells us, though, that instead of turning the boat around and going somewhere else, he had compassion for them and healed their sick.

There are many times while grieving when we just want to go somewhere and be alone, only to be met with responsibilities that demand our immediate attention. There are times when our lives can't completely slow down, even though we have just endured immense trauma. Our people, our jobs, and our homes all keep moving, and we want to push them all to the side. But Jesus showed us what to do in those moments.

He showed us in his time here on earth that there must be balance in our grief—that it's OK to take moments to weep for the people we love (as he wept for Lazarus) but that we also must keep our eyes fixed on heaven and eternity. In the moments of John's death, Lazarus's death, and his grief in the garden of Gethsemane, we see that Jesus kept his mind focused on the call that God gave him. He kept his eyes on the finish line and showed us that we are to do the same.

We will continue (just as Jesus did) to have responsibilities that we cannot always push to the side. But Jesus taught us that our grief is what makes us capable of looking at those responsibilities through a different lens. One of the beautiful things God creates from the ashes of death is a different view of the world. The reality of death and heaven is now at the forefront of our minds, and we therefore have a stronger fire in our bellies to share with others the truth of the cross and the hope that is ours.

Let us seize the opportunity, just as Jesus did, to let our grief empower us for ministry.

OUR GRIEF IS DIFFERENT

> We do not want you to be uninformed about those who sleep in death, so that you do not grieve like the rest of mankind who have no hope.
> —1 Thessalonians 4:13

Our grief is different from the rest of the world's. And that's because even though we hurt and ache tremendously, we also know this life is not the end. We have a hope and a certainty that is different. There are so many people who spend their entire lives on earth not knowing what happens after death, and for many, it's lonely and heart-wrenching. But because of his resurrection, we have the ability to live our lives in a completely different way. Because of Christ, we are able to lift our heads up off our pillows and keep moving forward. We are able to pick up the pieces of our shattered lives and come alongside God as he builds something from them. And we are able to obtain *joy* in the midst of life's worst moments. All because we know this is not the end, for us and for our babies.

When you grieve the loss of your baby, you are not only beginning the path to healing, but you are also *honoring* God. You are honoring him by acknowledging the preciousness of what he brought to life in you, and you are praising him by boasting of the love you had, and will always have, for the life he created inside of you. What a gift this is not only to the Lord but to your baby as well. You are celebrating your baby's life, however short it may have been, and you are giving glory to the Creator by acknowledging that every single life he creates is worthy.

Tune out the voices that tell you it's not OK, let the truth of what Scripture says about grieving resonate deeply, and give your heart permission to grieve.

NOTES

1. Noelle Mirabella, "Noelle Mirabella Photography," Facebook, July 11, 2021. Emphasis added.
2. Lucas Morgan, "Grief and 'Rising Cairn' by Celeste Roberge," *Seven-Ponds* (blog), February 17, 2019, https://blog.sevenponds.com/soulful-expressions/grief-and-rising-cairn-by-celeste-roberge.
3. Anette Kersting and Birgit Wagner, "Complicated Grief after Perinatal Loss," *Dialogues in Clinical Neurosciences* 14, no. 2 (2012): 187–94, https://doi.org/10.31887/DCNS.2012.14.2/akersting.

CHAPTER THREE

Bruises

September 9, 2018

Nobody warned me about laughing for the first time after losing him.

That guilt pierced straight through me. How in the world can laughing make you feel so terrible? I don't even remember what I was laughing about, but not even a tenth of a second after I started, a pit formed in my stomach, and tears welled up in my eyes.

You feel so much guilt about feeling happiness or joy after they're gone because you feel like it means you're moving on and forgetting them. It feels like you're dishonoring them. You tell yourself that you shouldn't be happy or laughing because they aren't here, and so the first time it happens, it completely wrecks you. And then you pinball back and forth from wanting to heal and move forward and laugh again to feeling immense guilt about wanting to heal and move forward and laugh again.

***

It can be incredibly hard to accept the way other people grieve or don't grieve the loss of our babies. Although we may have some people who offer full support by acknowledging the life of our daughter or son and who understand that we are walking through immense and heavy grief for an unknown period of time, there will also be other people in our lives who seem to either fall off the face of the earth during that time or say some of the most hurtful and insensitive things imaginable.

It's hard to know how to respond in those situations and hard to understand why some people react the way they do. I have learned, however, that people's responses to pregnancy loss stem from many different influences and circumstances, including what society says regarding it.

In many places, pregnancy loss is considered a taboo subject. It has been something that women have been told to keep quiet about and sweep under the rug. My question was *why*. Why is it something that most people "just don't talk about"? And what has led to generations of parents feeling the need to cover up and hide the loss of their babies?

There is even a general understanding in society to wait and announce a pregnancy until after the highest risk of loss is gone (usually after the first trimester) just in case loss occurs. That doesn't make sense to me. If a mother were to lose her baby, doesn't it make more sense for there to be a community gathered around her to support her as opposed to her experiencing it alone?

After researching a little bit about the history of pregnancy loss, I felt like I gained a better understanding of why it has become so stigmatized. Although this book doesn't dive into all of it, the history of pregnancy loss is very complex, with many different factors affecting and influencing the way society has come to view the subject. And these factors are what have contributed to so many women feeling the need to cover up and hide their losses.

The first factor has to do with a person's cultural beliefs. A person's culture, whether they currently live in it or were raised in it, highly influences their attitudes, opinions, thoughts, and behaviors regarding pregnancy loss. This might include things like mothers being pushed to move forward quickly after their loss, or it might mean that they experience shame for grieving an early miscarriage.

And *many* cultures and countries do not encourage the expression of feelings and emotions, especially sad ones. Many men and women are discouraged from crying or told to do so in private, which isolates mothers who desperately need support after their losses.

Another factor that has influenced the way society today talks about (or doesn't talk about) miscarriage is the historical lack of medical knowledge surrounding life in the womb. The lack of understanding and resources in the past led to some very peculiar beliefs about pregnancy in general that still carry through to today, the biggest being at what point life begins.

There have always been conflicting views about when human life begins in the womb that are still present today, with some believing that life begins at conception, some believing it doesn't begin until a mother feels the baby kick, and some believing life begins only after the baby is born.

Part of this confusion is because it was difficult to see or recognize a formed body in the tissues of an early miscarriage. And so, many physicians and mothers in eighteenth- and nineteenth-century America, for example, described early miscarriages as "false pregnancies" and had very little understanding of their meaning.[1] You can imagine how this led to misconceptions about when life actually began in utero that carried on through many generations. But in the nineteenth century, physicians diligently began studying embryology and discovered more and more about each stage of development and could therefore see that there was in fact a living human being in early pregnancy.[2] (We'll take a deeper look at how we know life begins at conception in Chapter Six.)

Religion is another factor that influences how people respond to a mother's loss. Some religions hold unborn life in high regard while others do not. And so there will be some people who do not believe that your baby's life had value and therefore won't understand or validate your grief. That includes some Christians as well. Someone's understanding of Scripture (or deficit of understanding) will affect what they say to grieving mothers.

And the last factor is an ideology that dates back to ancient civilizations; it's the belief that a woman's worth is measured by her ability to reproduce. Dating back to biblical times, being barren was considered a disgrace not only for Israelite women but for Hittite, Greek, and other populations of women as well. A childless wife risked being disdained or disowned by her husband and in-laws.[3] And this thought continued for generation after generation. Even women in eighteenth- and nineteenth-century America were told that mothering should be their lifestyle and only occupation and that if they did not produce children, they failed in their roles as women, which led to rejection for them both in their households and in society.[4]

This factor alone, I believe, has influenced so much of the stigma behind pregnancy loss. You can imagine that this is why so many women felt the need to hide their miscarriages, for fear of being ostracized from their husbands and from society.

And after generations of societies hammered this thought into the minds of both men and women, it's easy to see why we have generations now who still feel the need to cover up and hide their losses too.

Each of these factors, and more, have contributed to the way that many people respond to pregnancy loss. Their cultural beliefs, their knowledge and understanding of human life, and their views of a woman's role and purpose in society all affect the way they respond (or don't respond) to a mother who is grieving.

Some of those reactions are helpful and compassionate, but some of those responses end up being incredibly hurtful and are like pouring alcohol into an already open wound. And they can make us as mothers question the validity of our losses even more—and possibly even our faith in God.

Maybe you've had a few of these responses said to you:

"God just needed another angel."

"Don't be sad. You'll be a mom someday soon."

Anything starting with the words, "At least..."

"At least you know you can get pregnant."

"At least you have other children."

"Everything happens for a reason."

"God has a plan. / This is just a part of God's plan."

"You're still young."

"You can always have another."

"Miscarriages are so common."

The list can go on and on.

If you've found yourself frustrated and confused after hearing one of these statements (or any others), my encouragement to you is to always compare it with the truth of Scripture. Oftentimes people mean well (although there are some who truly don't mean well, unfortunately), but they don't realize the impact of what they're saying. They are trying to bring comfort to mothers but have no idea that what they are saying is actually not true and is more hurtful than helpful. Let's break these down and look at these statements with the backing of Scripture.

First, "God just needed another angel." The idea that our babies become angels when they die is a very common one. Many people say it to mothers to try to comfort them by painting beautiful pictures in their minds that their babies are now angels with wings in heaven. Some parents even make pictures of their children with angel wings placed on their backs or buy jewelry with angel wings on it to wear in memory of their babies that are no longer here. While the intention behind this idea is kind, the honest fact is this statement is not true.

It's not true for a few reasons. To begin with, God does *not need* anything. He is the sovereign God over the entire universe and does not have any needs whatsoever (Acts 17:25). He has no need to take our babies from earth up to heaven to populate it with more angels.

Secondly, our babies do not become angels when they go to heaven, and that's a beautiful thing! They are human beings just like you and I are, and we as humans are created in the image and likeness of God (Gen. 1:26). This means that we possess unique qualities and characteristics that reflect God's nature and are set apart from the rest of creation. A passage that causes confusion sometimes is Matthew 22:29–30, where Jesus explains we "will be *like* the angels" (emphasis mine), given the fact that in heaven we will not marry or be given in marriage, but it does not say that we will *become* angels. God created humans and angels to be different and do different things while on earth and in heaven (Ps. 8:5). After Christ returns, we will be coheirs with him (Gal. 4:7; Rom. 8:17), and we will be given brand new bodies in heaven that will "be like Jesus's glorious body" (Phil. 3:21; 2 Cor. 5:3). Our inheritance that we will receive includes new bodies, but they are not angelic bodies.

Another statement that people say that can be incredibly painful is "You'll be a mom someday soon." This implies that because you do not currently have a living child on earth, you are not, in fact, a mother. That is simply not true. The day that your child was conceived was the day that you became a mother. And even if you never have any other living children, you will always be a mother, even though your child is no longer here.

We would not tell a woman whose child died at two years of age, or twenty years of age, or fifty years of age that she was not a mother. And the same goes for women whose children died at five weeks of gestation, twenty weeks of gestation, or forty weeks of gestation. Their children simply died at some of the earliest stages of life.

Many of the other statements imply that the child you lost was somehow not significant in the "grand scheme" of things. The statements like "At least you have other children," "At least you know you can get pregnant," "Miscarriages are so common," "You can always have another," or "You're still young" all indicate that you need to just "look on the bright side" and simply be "thankful for what you do have." They imply that the baby you lost was not an individual and unique person and can easily be replaced. That's simply not true. Your baby was known by God before he or she was created (Jer. 1:5) and was fearfully and wonderfully made by him (Ps. 139:14). He or she will not and cannot ever be replaced.

The statements "Everything happens for a reason" and "God has a plan / This is just a part of God's plan" are probably some of the hardest statements to hear when you're experiencing tragedy. Kate Bowler says in her book *Everything Happens for a Reason: And Other Lies I've Loved*, "When someone is drowning, the only thing worse than failing to hand them a life preserver is handing them a reason."[5] This is so true. If tragedy has occurred, people don't need to hear the reason why, or that there's a reason at all. A mother who has just lost her baby doesn't need to hear that it must just be a part of God's plan. No, in that moment what they need is someone to hold them up and keep them from drowning.

Yes, God does have a plan, and he has had that plan since before the creation of the world. Being omniscient and therefore knowing that sin and death would enter the world and we as people would need redemption from it, he sent his Son to defeat sin and death, once and for all. And God is completely sovereign over that plan. He is sovereign over every part of our lives. There's not a single raindrop that hits the ground, or blade of grass that grows taller, or ant that digs a tunnel without the Lord commanding it to happen (Job 37:6; Ps. 89:9). And in his sovereignty, he has appointed a time for each person to be born and to die (Ps. 139:16; Eccles. 3:1–2; Job 14:5). As much as we would like for it to be, that time is not for our choosing.

The hard question then is, If God is sovereign over everything, why did he allow my baby to die? Why was my baby's appointed time to die so soon? What was the "reason" for God allowing this? These questions are absolutely valid ones, and they're ones that I have wrestled with God about too. And the truth is, no one on earth has the exact answer. It's important to note that when God allows things to happen here on earth, he isn't approving of it, and he isn't sitting back as a spectator, watching all of it unfold, seeing how/if we figure it out. Instead, he is actively involved in every part of our lives, constantly pursuing us, and continually bringing good from the evil of this world. In his creation of the world, there were some things we were not designed to know and understand. But what helped me when contemplating these questions was being reminded that his plan also allowed the persecution, ridicule, abuse, shame, and ultimately death of his own Son.

I've often thought about the millions of other ways that God could have fulfilled the redemption story of his people. And not a single one of them had anything to do with his own Son's excruciating death on a cross, let alone his own Son's death at all. So why did the God of the universe choose for everything to unfold the way that it did?

We don't have all the answers, and we won't until glory, but we can rest in the fact that God is not asking us to walk through something he hasn't also walked through himself. We can rest in the truth that he brings beauty from ashes and will one day restore all that has been broken in a place where death will no longer be a part of the picture. Because of his sovereignty, we don't have to know all the answers. Just as a child trusts in their parent when they can't fully understand every concept, we can trust in our Father now, knowing that one day we will understand.

No matter what hurtful remarks anyone else says to you, remember these three things:

- Your baby was a real person, unlike any other person who has ever lived or will ever live, and was created by the sovereign God of the universe.

- Your baby is in heaven, not as an angel, but as the person God created them to be, and will be given a new body that will be like Christ's.
- You became a mother the day your baby was conceived, and you will always be a mother to that child for the rest of your days.

(Chapter Five takes an in-depth look at how we know the above statements are true.)

It's frustrating and heartbreaking to hear some of the heart-wrenching things mothers have been told after the loss of their babies. One woman I spoke with told me her mother said this to her after losing her daughter very unexpectedly at thirty-four weeks: "I don't understand why you're so upset. She wasn't a real person. You need to get over this and move on."

We cannot help the way that others feel or what they say about our loss. The only thing that we can control is how we respond to it. This does *not* mean that we disregard what they say or the way it makes us feel when they say it. And it doesn't mean that we push our feelings aside and ignore them.

But we do get to make a choice about how we react to what people say.

What I came to understand was that not everyone was going to grieve Asher's death the same way, and some people weren't going to grieve it at all, much less acknowledge it.

But their responses did not dictate what my response was.

I learned to modify my expectations of how others responded to the news of my loss. For example, when I walked into a situation, I had very little expectations of the type of condolences we would receive, and I would remind myself that ultimately it didn't matter if we received any at all. What that helped me do was take any type of response that came and not be disappointed in any way. In other words, if I went in expecting big, I was let down big, and vice versa.

By no means did I do this perfectly. I still had moments where I thought certain people would say or do more than they did, and sometimes parts of me were let down when they didn't. But God reminded me that I must separate what people say and do from the *truth*. He reminded me to compare what someone said or did against the truth of Scripture, just like we have to do with everything else in our lives. If someone calls you unworthy, dumb, or unimportant, you contrast that with what God calls you. God calls you worthy, loved, chosen, and important enough to die for (Matt. 10:29-31; 1 Pet. 2:9; John 3:16). We have to do the same with what others say about us and about our babies, and we must keep ourselves grounded in that.

God also helped me give grace to others, knowing they probably

- really do have good intentions behind what they are saying and are trying to make me feel better,
- don't know the truth of Scripture to respond with a completely accurate statement, and
- have never been taught how to handle death or talk to someone who has experienced the loss of a baby.

That last one, I think, is the reason for the majority of the hurtful responses people make.

I think we as humans have developed an automatic reflex that makes us think we have to instantly make things better the moment someone tells us about a death or something terrible that's happened. Some of that comes from a good place, where people are deeply hurting for the other person and want to alleviate their pain, but I think we often do this because we are uncomfortable with grief and heartache. We don't know how to handle it, and it's easier to just say a "one-liner," "fix" it, and be done with it. It's not easy to sit in the muck and mud of life with someone. It's messy and uncomfortable.

But it's what people need.

Having done that myself in the past, but now having walked through heavy and intense grief, I want to help other people learn to resist that urge and just be in the moment and sit in the grief with whoever needs it. We need to learn how to be pillars of support that people can lean on when they get weary.

We especially as grieving parents need to teach others how to do this, how to let others know it's OK to let someone talk about their loss or their grief and *not* always have an answer or a way to fix it.

We simply need to be a listening ear.

We need to be someone they can trust with their emotions so they know they can come to us. There is power in just being in a room with someone who is hurting. You don't even have to say a single word, but your presence can make all the difference in the world. In that moment, they know they are not alone and that someone cares.

So many people have never been taught how to handle death and grief, and therefore it intimidates them—especially this particular type of grief. And I believe the only way to change that is by the people who have experienced it stepping up and lovingly declaring the truth regarding it. And part of that needs to include helping others understand that while they might be trying to be helpful, they are saying things that are actually hurtful.

I believe when the time is right, us mothers who have gone through this are the ones who can share the truth about how hurtful some statements can be, and we can therefore help change the narrative that so many mothers hear. There will be times when we can correct people and explain the truth to them and lead them back to Scripture so they hopefully won't say the same thing and possibly cause hurt to a different grieving mother. We can help them word their statements differently and ask different questions.

For example, here are some alternative statements and questions that we can share with other people that will hopefully help make talking about pregnancy loss a little easier:

- Instead of asking, "How many kids do you have?" say, "Tell me about your family."
- Instead of saying, "You can always have another baby," ask, "Do you want to talk about your baby?"
- Instead of "Everything happens for a reason," say, "I'm so sorry this happened."
- Instead of "Don't be sad," say, "I'm here for you."

One of the ways you can start a hard conversation with someone is by saying this: "I know that you likely mean well when you say that, but here is how what you just said is actually very hurtful." This doesn't attack them in any way, but it just makes them mindful of something they might not have been aware of. Their world is not like ours. They've never experienced this hurt and don't fully understand all they are saying. They don't know that certain questions are incredibly hard for grieving mothers to answer.

Still to this day, one of the hardest questions for me to answer is

"How many children do you have?"

In all truth, it's an innocent question. But for any mother who has lost a child (or more than one child), it can be hard to answer. I've heard this from mothers in all stages of life—mothers who have lost babies, mothers who have lost teenagers, and mothers who have lost adult children. And it doesn't matter if they lost them yesterday or twenty years ago; it's still a hard question to answer.

In the earliest moments of my grief, my answer depended highly on where my emotions were that day. If it had been a particularly triggering day, then I knew I could only answer with "two" instead of "three"; otherwise, I'd risk breaking down in tears. My answer depended on whether I wanted to go through the emotional roller coaster of explaining our third and possibly receive a negative response from someone.

But the worst part about that question was the guilt that ate me alive on the days when I chose to only answer "Two." I walked away feeling like I had betrayed my son, like me answering the question that way made him all of a sudden not part of our family or made it as if he never existed. That wasn't true, and deep down I knew that. Regardless, guilt poured over me every time.

I want to emphasize that it's not wrong if you don't tell every person about your baby/babies that are no longer here. I fully believe that the Holy Spirit will give us discernment on what is wise to share each time we have a conversation with someone and the opportunity to talk about our babies. I have certainly met some people whom I could tell right away it wouldn't be wise for me to share my story with.

I believe he will also help us to know whether to share the truth in those moments when someone needs to hear it or give us discernment to know when we need to just walk away. This doesn't necessarily mean physically walking away while someone's talking but knowing when to let someone's hurtful comment or statement go in one ear, process it, understand that it's not true, and then let it go right back out the other ear. And then know that it's OK to just let that person and that comment go and walk away without giving any guidance.

But sometimes God will provide an opportunity to gently share with other people the hurt that comes with what they've just said and will provide a beautiful platform for healing and help for so many people. Many times when I've shared how some of the statements or questions someone has asked me or others are actually hurtful, people have responded so well with "I had no idea" or "I am so sorry, I never thought of it like that" or "I'm sorry, that's not at all what I meant." And from there, they know how to say their words differently around the next grieving mom they talk with.

My biggest encouragement to you is to not let the hard conversations scare you away from the good ones. In the moments when you know it's wrong, walk away, but in the moments when you know it's right, share with others about your children who are no longer here. There are so many hurting women who have felt so scared to share their babies with other people, but when others open up and share their stories, a weight is lifted off, a door is opened, and a bridge is made, and then they feel like they can share their story too. And the more women do that, the less taboo pregnancy loss becomes, and the community of grieving mothers is strengthened tremendously.

* * *

One of the questions I get asked often is

> "What can I do to help a mother
> who's just lost her baby?"

And more specifically,

"What do I *say* to a mother who has just lost her baby?"

What I've come to understand is that there isn't much you can say. And what I mean by that is that while technically, yes, there are many Scripture verses, comforting words, quotes, and so on that you could share with her, the truth is, for mothers whose loss is very recent, most of those words will go in one ear and out the other and likely won't be helpful right away. Even the most well-put-together sentences can't take away the immediate and excruciating pain of losing her child.

But the one thing that will mean the most to her is to acknowledge her baby. Let her know that her baby was loved and cherished and will be remembered even though he or she is gone. If you are talking with a mother you don't know very well, but she has shared her loss with you, one of the best questions you can ask her is "Would you like to tell me about your baby?" This lets her know she has a safe space to tell you her story if she wants and allows her to process some of her grief by verbalizing it.

Other things that can help her are

- Making meals for her and her family. This is such a weight off her shoulders, especially if she has other family members that she cares for.
- Praying (either directly with her or for her).
- Volunteering to do something for her that could lighten her load. I say volunteering instead of asking her what

she needs because, oftentimes, mothers who are grieving (and really, anyone who is grieving) have no idea what they need or don't need. If you were to ask them "What can I do to help you?" they likely would have no idea or might feel shame accepting help. Use discernment to figure out when to offer and what is appropriate. But offering things like watching her other children for a few hours, setting up a meal plan, hiring a cleaning service for an afternoon, picking up groceries for her, and so on can all help tremendously.

- Sending her a heartfelt gift. There are *wonderful* resources now that make keepsakes for mommas who have lost babies. Anything from jewelry to sonogram paintings to weighted stuffed bears can mean the world to a hurting mother. (I have provided a list of companies in the back of this book that sell different gifts.)
- Continuing to check in on her. One of the things that meant the most to me was when people continued to text or call here and there just to check in on me. They knew that the pain didn't just magically go away and that I was still hurting weeks and months later, and they took the time to check in and make sure I was OK.

* * *

Every person you encounter is going to grieve the death of your baby differently, and their reasons will stem from a million different things. Unfortunately, some of those encounters will bring pain, but God will also intentionally bring you other people, and speak through them, to bring you comfort and remind you of the truth of him and the truth about the babies that die during pregnancy. Those people will be beacons of light in the midst of an overwhelming darkness. Cherish them, thank God for them, and keep them close to you.

Others are going to say things with good intentions, trying to bring you comfort and hope without understanding the extent of what they are saying, and they may cause a lot of pain. And as a result, you may walk away with more wounds and bruises to add to your list.

Because society has made pregnancy loss a taboo subject, hidden under the rug for many generations, we now have a community of people with no idea how to respond to a mother who has lost her baby. But we have the opportunity to begin changing the narrative and depiction surrounding this loss. We have the opportunity to bring beauty from ashes and the chance to share truth regarding the lives of our babies and all the babies that die during pregnancy. Use those opportunities that the Lord places before you to share the story of your baby with others, and remember no matter what response you get from anyone, your compass is always the truth of the Bible.

NOTES

1 Shannon Withycombe, *Lost: Miscarriage in Nineteenth-Century America* (New Brunswick, NJ: Rutgers University Press, 2019), 9.
2 Withycombe, 7.
3 Roy B. Zuck, *Precious in His Sight: Childhood and Children in the Bible* (Eugene, OR: Wipf and Stock, 2012), 47, 50.
4 Withycombe, *Lost*, 6.
5 Kate Bowler, *Everything Happens for a Reason: And Other Lies I've Loved* (New York: Random House, 2018), 170.

CHAPTER FOUR

Till Death Do Us Part

August 3, 2018

Today I've felt lonely. At least, I think I have. I'm not really sure because I don't know that I've ever felt true loneliness before. Usually, I don't mind being by myself, and there are times when I prefer it. But today the loneliness has almost driven me crazy. Austin has just left with Liam to go to New York, and so it's just Graham and me.

I can't figure out what to do with myself. I want to start doing something to keep my mind off things and to feel productive, but I also feel guilty doing anything at all because I don't want to forget him and feel like I'm "moving on." I'm extremely restless, and my mind is spinning in a million directions.

I've been surrounded by so many people who love and care about me that I don't understand how or why I feel lonely. It doesn't make sense. But a thought ran through my head today as I was driving home: my loneliness might be intentional. It might be God's way of asking me to let him in.

* * *

I knew in the weeks following Asher's death that Austin and I would grieve him differently—partly because we have grieved other deaths differently before, but also because he and I were created differently. Our minds were created to think differently, and our bodies were created to do different things.

Yes, in some ways, that is as simple as it sounds; he is a male, and I am a female. My body was made to physically carry and nourish Asher for the months he was inside of me. Austin's body was not. But I'm also talking on an even deeper level about the unique characteristics God created in each of us, the specific ways that our brains think and process things. Because throughout our years of marriage, he and I have learned that they are very different.

For example, I usually need time to process things and filter situations out in my head. Austin prefers for things to get resolved quickly and to handle a situation in that moment, not hours or days later. Neither way is "right" or "wrong," but it is most certainly not the same. And it can be hard to work through conflicts that arise without understanding the other person's way of handling certain situations.

We know that God designed differences between men and women for a reason. But sometimes it's hard to step back, look at your spouse, and see them for who they are and for who God created them to be and not for who you want them to be. Especially when your marriage hits crossroads and difficult situations. Grief after losing a baby is no exception to that rule.

In navigating our marriage after loss, what became so valuable for me was learning some of the different factors that can influence how grief displays itself in men versus women. Some of the factors are more obvious than others, and each one does not necessarily apply to every marriage or relationship. But when we take the time to consider what influences the conflicting differences between men's and women's grief, we can gain more compassion and understanding for the other.

Let's examine some of the most common factors.

BIOLOGICAL DIFFERENCES

In God's perfect and meticulous design of men and women, he created our physical bodies to not only look different but function differently and do different things as well. That design was intentional and necessary. For example, we as women were designed to carry our babies from the moment they are conceived and experience all the physical changes that come with pregnancy. We feel their every move—every kick, jolt, stretch, and hiccup, and every time they turn and flip-flop. And each time that happens, a memory is formed in our brains. Additionally, the hormones in our bodies change to bring about an emotional connection, which creates a truly unique bond that mothers and babies get to experience. And eventually, our minds and bodies go through giving birth. That birth looks different for each woman, but that birth is an extraordinary experience that builds an even stronger connection to our babies, even if our babies aren't born alive.

These specific biological realities emphasize the fact that the bond mothers form with their babies during pregnancy is usually stronger than the father's bond. It has to be by design.

And so when it comes to experiencing grief after the loss of a baby, because women have a much deeper connection, their grief is usually much greater than men's.

But there are also other biological factors, specifically regarding the brain, that influence how and why men and women typically express grief differently. If you were to look at a male and female brain side by side, physically, they would look very similar (although male brains are typically about 10 percent larger than women's). The difference between them is found in their functionality. When studying the brain, scientists have discovered variations in different activity centers of the brain while men and women were performing physical or cognitive tasks (like logic and reasoning, language skills, and problem-solving) or while experiencing different emotions.[1]

One of those functional differences is in communication. Women tend to be able to verbalize their emotions much easier than men, and studies have given us evidence as to why.

The brain is divided into left and right hemispheres. The left hemisphere deals more with analytics, logic, and details, while the right hemisphere is described as more creative, intuitive, and holistic. The left hemisphere is primarily dominant for men, while women tend to shift back and forth drawing on both the left *and* the right hemispheres. Women have the ability to do this because the connective tissue between the two hemispheres is thicker in women than it is in men, and so women have a greater connection between verbal capacity and emotions. Men, instead of verbalizing what they are feeling, tend to describe their grief through their physical bodies—experiencing tightness in their chest, feeling like their stomach dropped, or imagining there's a knot in their throat.[2]

Studies have also shown that the limbic system is more active in women. This part of the brain is involved with bonding, nesting, and emotions. And one of the brain's "worry centers," the anterior cingulate gyrus (or ACG), has been shown to be more active in women than in men.[3]

And when it comes to the production of tears, there is a biological reason that women tend to cry more often than men. It has to do with the hormone prolactin. Prolactin is instrumental in the production of emotional tears and is produced in much higher amounts in women than in men. Additionally, having larger amounts of testosterone (which is higher in men than women) has been shown to inhibit the production of tears.[4]

So when comparing a mother's grief to a father's, there are multiple biological factors that could play a part in why it looks so different. Our bond as mothers with our babies is truly unique. We experience so much more during pregnancy than men do. And functionally, our brains are very different from men's. Not better or worse, not less or more, just different. And so it makes sense that our pain can sometimes feel deeper and more intense than the father's pain. And it makes sense that our grief is unlike theirs.

We have pain and memories they never experienced. And although we might outwardly express our pain more than men, it's important to remember that the absence of tears or verbal expression does not equate to the absence of pain. In other words, even if your husband does not cry or doesn't have as much to say about the loss of your baby, it does not mean that he isn't feeling pain or isn't grieving.

HISTORICAL DIFFERENCES

The second factor that can influence how men and women grieve pregnancy loss is historical differences. Historically, men have been seen as the protectors and providers of the family.

Therefore, many men will think that their primary role in a crisis situation is to care for their loved ones and protect them from further pain.

But sometimes what can happen is that taking on the role of protector can override a man's emotional experience of loss. Men know they *have* to push their own feelings aside so that they can remain strong for their wives. And a lot of times, this results in them not talking about what's happened because that's the only way they know how to remain strong.

The role of women throughout history, however, has been to nurture, to provide care, to seek out others as sources of comfort, and to share feelings with each other. And so what comes naturally most of the time and is comforting for us as women is to talk about it.

You can see how easily these two different historical norms might cause confusion or conflict in a marriage when not understood. They are two opposite reactions and ways of managing grief.

SOCIAL AND FAMILIAL INFLUENCES

The last factor has to do with society's influence on our lives. Much of the way we think, act, and feel is shaped by what our society tells us we should be thinking, doing, and feeling. And many of those social influences are impacted by what has been done throughout history.

For example, boys in previous generations were discouraged from crying, and men who showed any kind of public display of emotion were often not socially accepted and were seen as weak. This societal norm was accepted in many families and became what was taught from generation to generation. For many of us, what we were taught, how we were raised, and our early life experiences play massive roles in our lives and impact how we handle death and grief.

Maybe this specific societal influence was true for your husband, and he grew up in a family where showing emotion was deeply discouraged, or he was only allowed to show good emotions like joy and happiness, but sadness and frustration were unacceptable. Maybe he was told that showing sadness was a sign of weakness and that he should push whatever it is that's making him sad aside and pretend it didn't happen. This way of thinking might be all that he's ever known, and therefore it is the only way that he knows how to respond to what happens in his life now.

As a result of these factors (but also, oftentimes, out of love), many men express their grief by primarily focusing on supporting their wives through their grief, doing everything they can to make the situation better for them.

Each of these three factors—biological, historical, and social—all impact when, how, or even *if* men grieve at all. They show us why their grief is often more outwardly reserved: because of the way their brains and bodies are wired and because of the way they were likely influenced or taught how to handle this. As you think about your own marriage, consider how each of these might play a role in your husband's grief, and let that knowledge aid in your understanding and compassion for how he expresses that grief.

* * *

Because men's brains function more logically, and they see things for what they are, they tend to *accept* the truth of situations sooner and subsequently begin moving forward much quicker than women. Austin, for example, accepted that Asher was gone and was not meant to live on this earth for longer than he did far sooner than I accepted it. I personally had a harder time submitting to that reality, thinking there must have been some kind of mistake and questioning why God would allow it. My brain knew the truth of the situation—it knew that Asher was gone and wasn't coming back—but my heart just couldn't truly accept it. And it was hard for me to understand how Austin could.

There's a passage in Scripture that I believe is a great example of the very logical and straightforward way that many men grieve. It's the story of David and Bathsheba found in 2 Samuel.

In chapters 11 and 12, we are told that King David conceived a child with a woman named Bathsheba through adultery and then subsequently had Bathsheba's husband murdered so that he could marry her. God then tells David, through the prophet Nathan, that as a result, the child they conceived will become sick and die.

After the child is born and becomes ill, David is so distraught that he refuses to eat and "lay[s] all night on the ground" (2 Sam. 12:16 ESV). And then when the child does die, his servants are "afraid to tell him" because they were afraid he would "do himself some harm" (2 Sam. 12:18 ESV). But after David understood that his son had died, he got himself off the floor, cleaned himself up, went and worshiped the Lord, and then ate a meal.

His servants were incredibly puzzled by this. Verse 21 says they questioned him, asking, "What is this thing you have done? You fasted and wept for the child while he was alive; but when the child died you arose and ate food." They weren't expecting the king to be so calm and seemingly passive regarding his son's death, especially considering how tormented he was before. But when David explains himself to his servants, he makes it clear that he understands his child is gone and that there is nothing he can do to bring him back. He says to them that one day he "will go to him," but right now, "he will not return to me" (2 Sam. 12:23).

There is so much to be examined in this particular account in biblical history, and I talk more about it in Chapter Five, but the one thing I want to bring attention to is how David responds after his child's death.

There is no question about how deep David's love is for his son. When the child was alive and sick, he lay on the floor, wouldn't get up, and refused to eat. He never stopped praying, all the while knowing what the Lord had already declared (Nathan had spoken for the Lord)—the child *would* die. And he was so distressed that his servants didn't even want to tell him the child had died because they were afraid he would harm himself.

But as soon as he finds out the child has died, his response is very matter-of-fact, and his thinking is decidedly direct. And I found this so similar to the way many men can at times acknowledge the loss of their babies (and possibly loss in general). They pick themselves up, accept that there is nothing more that can be done, and begin moving forward. That doesn't, however, mean there is an absence of pain. Scripture doesn't tell us directly, but I can imagine the king had many more thoughts and emotions about his son. Pain inevitably still lingers, but the acceptance of reality is now at the forefront.

As women, however, this very straightforward response is hard to understand. We interpret that behavior as men not caring, and we wonder how they can just begin moving forward as if nothing has happened. And that lack of understanding can sometimes lead to hurt in a marriage. Austin and I absolutely had those moments. The story that I share next is about one of those instances in particular for Austin and me, but we also got to watch God redeem it in such a beautiful way.

AUGUST 1, 2018

In the first few days after we lost Asher, Austin was different than I had ever seen him. He immediately jumped into the "protector" role and did everything he could to provide support for me. He would constantly check on me and see if there was anything I needed, be it physically, emotionally, or spiritually. And he literally held me up in the moments when I felt like I couldn't stand.

We both talked with each other constantly. We could look at each other's faces and see when the other was thinking hard about something, making sure to always ask, "What are you thinking right now?" And we made it a priority to constantly share our hearts and minds with each other.

Then, after a few days, the talking slowed a little. It didn't completely stop, but it wasn't constant like before. Austin was at a place in his grief where he didn't need to talk as much anymore. Not because his pain was gone by any means, but because he didn't need to continue to verbalize as much as I did; he needed to grieve differently now. He needed to get out and do things. He had always been someone who got restless being inside for long periods of time.

We still made it a priority to talk and share our hearts and minds; we knew how vital that was in working through this. But I tried hard not to take it personally when he didn't have as much to say as I did or when he didn't seem to be affected by the same things that were still affecting me.

And then one day, after about two weeks had passed, he came and said he wanted to talk with me about something. We previously had plans to attend his family's annual reunion in New York that weekend, before our lives had been flipped upside down. He told me that he still wanted to go and asked if I was OK with that. He offered to take Liam, our eldest son, so that I would not have to take care of both boys by myself.

At first, I didn't really know how to respond. Part of me was just surprised that he was even still considering going. I answered him very honestly and told him that I did not want him to go. I told him that I needed him here with me, that just physically having him here with me made me feel safe. It made me feel like I could handle all this. But I think, subconsciously, it made me feel like I wasn't alone. At that point, I had hit true loneliness for the first time ever in my life, and in my mind, if Austin was gone, I was scared it might only get worse.

After we discussed it for a while, I told him that if he really wanted to go, he could, but I reiterated that I really didn't want him to. I think I wrestled with it for so long because part of me felt deep down that getting out of the house was probably something he needed to do for his grief. It was something that would help him heal, even though it might make it harder for me. But even recognizing that, I was still hurt when he told me he had made the decision he was going to go.

I was angry and confused. I felt like my pain didn't matter to him anymore, and I didn't know what to think. I remember crying out to God in confusion, asking him how in the world he could even be thinking about leaving me, especially after I had asked him not to. I expected him to be there for me, but he wasn't.

But God, being the loving Father that he is and knowing my aching heart, pulled me in close to him and showed me that I was expecting Austin to be and do more than he should.

I was expecting him to continue handling this exactly the way that I needed. Not also the way that *he* needed.

The honest truth is that we both did what was right in that moment. We both spoke truth to each other. I verbalized the truth to him, that I needed him here with me and didn't want him to go. I didn't lie about it or try to cover anything up. And he spoke truth in that moment as well, stating that he needed to get out of the house. We each had two separate needs.

Austin had been putting so many of my needs before his for the previous two weeks, but I didn't know how to put that into perspective at the time. I was so overcome with fear and loneliness and confusion still that I felt the only way for me to be OK was to have him by my side.

And it's in these moments where grief in marriage can be so hard and complex—where choices have to be made, and sometimes you don't know what choice is right. You as a mother are so overcome with heartbreak and exhaustion and physical pain that being asked to think about and consider someone else's needs seems overwhelming and impossible. And fathers are also overcome with heartbreak and grief while also trying to help support their wives in any way they can and navigate through any emotions they are feeling.

I am truly certain now, however, that God helps us make those difficult choices in those challenging moments. He knows when we are so overwhelmed and can't determine which way is up or down, and he speaks to us in different ways to guide us and direct us.

Austin, being who he is and who God created him to be, was never going to grieve the same way that I was or the way that I expected him to. Yes, in this instance, he did hurt me, and yes, in many ways, that hurt could have been prevented. But God used the time while Austin was gone to remind me of two very important things:

1. I cannot fully depend on Austin to carry me through my grief, and there will be times when he lets me down and times when I let him down.

2. God is the one who I need to be *fully* clinging to. He is the only one who can fully sustain me in the deepest parts of my grief. Not Austin, or anyone else.

Woven through the examples in Scripture, we learn that the people in our lives will sometimes fail us. Not a single one of them is perfect, and they are going to let us down—even the people who love us the most (Pss. 73:26, 118:8). And that's because they are people. They are human. They are imperfect. They are not God.

And that is why we can only *fully* depend on God, because he will never fail us (Luke 1:37; Ps. 145:13). Nor will he ever leave us or forsake us (Heb. 13:5; Deut. 31:6).

Bring your weary soul to him, lean on him, and let him carry you.

Sometimes that looks like falling down on your knees and saying, "Lord, I literally cannot do this. I don't know where to go from here, and even if I did, I don't know that I would have the strength to pick myself up to do it."

I remember getting to this place. It was an exhaustion I had never experienced before, and it hit me in waves during my grief. And I felt like the only cure would be for me to go to a remote island in the middle of nowhere with no responsibilities or anyone to take care of, where I could sleep and rest as much as I needed. The honest truth is, that can't happen for most of us.

But in the moments when I fully surrendered all of it to him, he supernaturally gave me what I needed. I had energy that I didn't have the day before, even without getting any more sleep or rest. I had patience and compassion for those around me that came out of nowhere. I had strength that I could not have mustered up on my own. He led me to the words in Scripture, or the people in my life that he would speak through, and he taught me new things about him that I had never known. He took my faith and grew it exponentially. He took my weakness and made it into strength.

There are times in our grief when we are going to be alone, even when we are surrounded by people who love us. I have learned in my journey that that's purposeful by God. Elijah knew what it was to be alone; Paul and Joseph knew too. Moses, Job, and so many more learned what it meant to be alone with God and sustained by God and God alone.

We cannot heal if we are solely dependent on people here on earth. It's not that they cannot or won't help us; they will. But they are limited as to what they can do. Max Lucado said in his book *A Love Worth Giving*,

> "God always allows us to feel the frailty of human love so that we'll appreciate the strength of His."[5]

If God allows solitude in your life, or if there are moments when you feel alone (even though you are surrounded by people), lean into the notion that he is using that loneliness to create a bridge to bring you closer to him, and my advice to you would be to run as quickly as you can across it.

***

I was told by multiple people after we lost Asher that Austin and I needed to make sure we worked very hard to keep our marriage healthy and strong because many couples end up divorced after the loss of a baby. When I first heard that, I couldn't even comprehend that that was a possibility.

"I have just lost my son, and now you're telling me I could lose my marriage as well?"

I knew they were coming from a good place, but that was one of the last things I wanted to hear in the midst of my grief. Any additional fear that I had regarding our lives at that point was heightened even more.

But I now know why they were saying it. I now know that it is absolutely true. Grief and loss put a *tremendous* amount of stress on a relationship, especially when the other person grieves very differently than you and you've never walked through that kind of agony together before.

Unfortunately, there is no single mathematical formula to follow guaranteeing a marriage free from any friction as you walk through loss. But there are a few things you can implement and avoid that can help tremendously when there are days that are tough.

One of the very first things that Austin and I did together was sit down and make a verbal declaration to do *everything* we could do to keep our marriage strong. We understood that we were going to have hard and challenging days but that those hard days didn't have to define our marriage. And at the ends of those days, even if hurtful things were said or done, we knew there was still a deep love for each other and a true desire to stay together.

Those hard days came and went; some were harder than others. But we each clung to the understanding that our love was still there—it was just buried underneath a mountain of pain.

The following is what we learned and what helped us the most as we navigated marriage after loss.

COMMUNICATE

I cannot stress this enough: the absolute number one thing that you both must work hard to do is communicate. We were told this by multiple people, and I can truly say how helpful it really is. I know this can seem like a big challenge for some, especially if you or your husband don't normally verbalize a lot of what you are thinking. But the only way for your husband to be able to know what is truly on your mind is for you to tell him (and vice versa).

This doesn't mean sitting in chairs across from each other and spending hours a day discussing every thought and feeling. But it does mean sharing when grief is hitting you hard and you need some space to try to process what you're feeling or determine what you should do. That allows each of you to know that any silence or short tone of voice or easy frustration is not directed at them or anything they have done but is just the symptom of something deeper.

As valuable as it would be, your husband cannot read your mind. He has no idea the amount of pain you are truly experiencing. He has no idea about the physical pain you're feeling (he has never endured that before) or the heaviness that comes with completing normal everyday things. He doesn't know that it's hard for you to want to go and do things because you feel guilty and feel like you are forgetting your baby or that it's hard for you to go to family or friend events knowing there is another woman there who is pregnant or has a newborn. Verbalize to him when you need certain things. There were multiple times when Austin was happy to do whatever was needed in a situation, but he would have had no idea that I needed it if I had not said anything to him.

The same goes for men as well. They usually do not verbalize as much as women, especially when they are grieving, so it can be easy to misunderstand your husband's grief when you don't know exactly what he's feeling or thinking. Sometimes you may have to initiate the conversation and just remind him that talking helps you to be able to aid him in whatever way he needs through his grief.

GET COUNSELING IF NEEDED

This can be individual counseling or marriage counseling. Sometimes even when we are taking the time we need to work through our grief, it can be hard to sort through everything we have experienced / are experiencing because our brains are so overwhelmed. This is especially helpful if either you or your husband (or both) have trouble communicating. Talking with a counselor can help you sort through it all. I have provided some resources in the back of this book on how to find Christian marriage counselors near you.

GIVE THE OTHER PERSON SPACE TO GRIEVE HOW THEY NEED

Whatever needs are said from one person to another, do what you can to make them happen. Austin needed to get out of the house. I needed to stay in the house. He needed to go and do; I needed to stay and just be. Verbalize each of those things to each other, and work together to respect the other's needs and find ways to meet them.

MODIFY EXPECTATIONS AND REMEMBER THAT NO ONE IS PERFECT

We cannot expect our husbands to be the ones to "fix" every problem. When we do that, we are setting our hopes up for failure because no one person on this earth can do that for us. Only Christ can. That also creates a tremendous amount of pressure for your husband that isn't fair to put on him. He cannot be everything you need in every moment of every day for the rest of your life. It's impossible. And you cannot be that for him either. The only person that can be that for us is Christ.

DEPEND ON GOD FIRST AND FOREMOST

Pour into God's scriptures, cry out to him in prayer, and be still and sit quietly in his presence every single day. That quiet time that you carve out just for him, whether it be in the earliest hours of the morning before the rest of the house is awake, right smack-dab in the middle of a hectic day, or in the moments before you fall asleep, allows you to quiet the rest of noise of the world and hear your Shepherd's voice more clearly. This is where your spirit will be renewed, and he will give rest to your weary soul.

GIVE GRACE UPON GRACE

If there is one thing I have learned in the ten years I have been married (nine of those also being a parent), it's that a lot of times, our reactions in stressful moments are often fueled by our feelings in that moment. Particularly exhaustion. I can't tell you the number of times when our conversations got heated because we were *just. plain. tired.* And grief, in particular, is exhausting.

There were many times when hurtful things were said or done, and it required us to step back, see what was really going on in that moment, and give the other person grace. Had Austin gone through something stressful at work that day, or had something triggered my grief? Practice recognizing or discovering the truth behind the frustration, and work hard to offer each other the grace needed for that moment.

* * *

I know that some of the mothers reading this have a husband who truly does not care about the loss of their babies. I'm sorry, momma, if this is you and what you are experiencing. It's heartbreaking when the people we rightfully expected to grieve with us and help us don't. I wish that I could wrap my arms around you, because I know there is a deep loneliness and isolation that you feel.

There could be a reason why your husband feels this way. It might be a lack of knowledge or understanding; he may not know or believe that life begins at conception and therefore doesn't believe that your baby had any significance. Or maybe he was never taught how to care for someone who's hurting and doesn't know how to comfort you, so he avoids it altogether. There could be many different factors that play into all of it. Ask God to reveal those to you and to your husband, and pray that in the meantime, God will lead him to the truth and also lead you to the people that will help you and comfort you in your grief.

* * *

The adversity in our lives, the hard things the Lord asks us to endure, create the most beautiful opportunities for God to grow us and strengthen us. They are what help us learn new things we didn't know before and develop strength and character within us.

This absolutely applies in our marriages too. Hard circumstances can grow and strengthen a marriage tremendously, but they can also break a marriage if hard work and effort are not put forth. As hard as it is walking through this together, always remember that trials in marriage are what harbor the deepest and strongest connections between you and your spouse. Each storm forces you to hammer an anchor deeper and deeper, and the result is that you are then prepared for the rest of the storms the two of you will face.

Take the time to understand the differences in the way that your husband grieves, respect them, and ask him to do the same. And just know that he was created differently and uniquely, so his grief will be different and unique too. Let your husband walk next to the Savior in his grief, and you walk on the other side of the Savior in yours. Let Christ be at the center of your marriage, meeting both of you exactly where you are and bringing healing to both of your aching hearts.

NOTES

1 Marek Glezerman, "Yes, There Is a Female and a Male Brain: Morphology versus Functionality," *Proceedings of the National Academy of Sciences* 113, no. 14 (2016): E1971, https://doi.org/10.1073/pnas.1524418113.
2 "Do Men Grieve?" Edward D. Lynch Funeral Home, Inc., accessed February 29, 2024, https://edwarddlynchfuneralhome.com/146/Do-Men-Grieve-.html.
3 "7 Differences between Male and Female Brains," Amen Clinics, https://www.amenclinics.com/blog/7-differences-between-male-and-female-brains/.
4 Lorna Collier, "Why We Cry," American Psychological Association, February 2014, https://www.apa.org/monitor/2014/02/cry.
5 Max Lucado, *A Love Worth Giving: Living in the Overflow of God's Love* (Nashville, TN: Thomas Nelson, 2006), 110.

CHAPTER FIVE

Certainty

July 18, 2018

I took him into my hands and brought him where I could see him clearly. Austin sat next to me and wrapped his arm around me, and we both sat in awe and wonder looking at our beautiful son.

Even though he was gone, I was so worried that somehow, I could still possibly hurt him. He was so small and fragile. It felt like even the slightest movement would injure him somehow.

I held him in front of me and began to study every part of him. The first thing I noticed was how much he looked like his father and eldest brother, Liam. Liam has so many of Austin's physical features, especially when it comes to his head shape and facial structure (Graham, our youngest, has more of my features), and at eighteen weeks, we could already see that Asher was going to favor Austin as well.

I took his tiny hand and placed it in mine. When I recognized just how small it was, I very carefully moved it so that only my finger held it up and I could get a closer look at it. That precious little hand fit perfectly over the tip of my finger. There were four fingers and a thumb, with fingernails perfectly positioned on each one. And every groove and facet of his knuckles had been carefully carved out.

I marveled at that hand, all the while knowing I would never feel it embrace mine. Not yet, at least.

I moved my gaze to his chest, observing his very recognizable rib cage. One by one, the ribs had formed, protecting his vital organs that just two days ago had been working full blast to keep him alive and growing. His skin was still transparent, and it allowed us to see his very detailed venous system. As thin as a single strand of hair, and meticulously woven together like a spider weaves its web, each vein connected with another exactly where it needed to.

He had perfectly formed kneecaps that were round, white, and exactly where they needed to be, and it was flawlessly evident that God had made him a boy.

At last, I came to his feet. Oh, those precious feet.

Measuring at only five-eighths of an inch, that little foot was no bigger than the size of a dime. All ten toes were accounted for, each with an unmistakable toenail and an arch and heel that were perfectly sculpted.

Every single part of him, down to the smallest molecule, was nothing less than a direct reflection of the Creator's hands. God is the Potter, and we are the clay (Isa. 64:8). Only He could make something so perfect.

I expected that moment to be full of tears, for me to not even be able to see him clearly because of all the weeping. But there was a peace over me that I still to this day cannot fully explain. It's what I now know is "the peace that passes all understanding" (Phil. 4:7).

There was a cloud over that room, and the presence of the Lord was palpable.

I looked at my son and couldn't help but smile. Because in that very first moment, all that I could see was the exquisiteness and perfection of what God had made—the beauty He created inside me, which I got the privilege of holding in my hands and witnessing with my own eyes.

With tears gently rolling down my face, I smiled knowing this wasn't the end. There would be a day when I would reach for that hand once again, feel it hold tightly to mine, and never have to let it go.

***

"IS MY BABY IN HEAVEN?"

I remember sitting on my couch in the deepest parts of my grief, desperate for God, searching every part of Scripture for answers that would bring me comfort and take the pain away and wishing the answer to this particular question was written right in front of me in bold, bright letters. I knew deep within my soul that the answer was "Yes, of course my son is in heaven. All babies go to heaven," but I couldn't tell you exactly where it said that in Scripture.

And I feel like there are many people today that feel the same. They know that they know, without a doubt, that our God would not send babies to hell, but they don't know *how* we know that and can't back it with Scripture. There's not necessarily a lot that's been taught from the pulpits in churches regarding it, and so I feel like grieving mothers are left wondering if their thoughts and feelings are actually true. On the other hand, I know there are also many mothers who have been told that their babies were not real people and are questioning if the existence of heaven and seeing their babies again one day is even a possibility.

What we as grieving mothers need are answers rooted in the truth of Scripture, not answers that merely make us or someone else feel better for the moment. Our emotions throughout this grief journey will wax and wane, but thankfully, the Word of God does not; it stays the same forever (Isa. 40:8; Ps. 119:89). So when answering this question, and all our questions regarding our babies, we need concrete answers from God himself.

But in order to answer this question, we must answer two other questions first:

1. "When does Scripture declare that life begins?"
2. "Does God value babies in the womb?"

The answers to those two questions determine a lot.

The question of when life begins is one of the most debated questions in the world, with answers varying from the moment of conception, to when the heart begins beating, to only when the baby can survive outside the womb or only when a baby takes its first breath after birth. But the answer to this question shapes the entirety of our grieving process. If life begins at any other time than conception, then that means for us as grieving mothers that *none* of our babies or only *some* of our babies were alive and more than just cells of tissue. That means *none* of us or only *some* of us are able to have hope of seeing our babies again and spending eternity with them. But is that what Scripture really shows us? In all that I have learned, it is not. It shows us that life begins at the moment of conception.

And so, if Scripture shows us that life begins at the moment of conception, the next question to ask is "Does God value that life in the womb?" We know that God has an indescribable love for us as humans. We are set apart from the rest of creation and have been created in the image and likeness of God himself and will one day rule with Christ in the new heaven and earth (Gen. 1:26-27; Rom. 8:17). But does that include the babies growing inside of us? Does God love them? Do they have value in his eyes?

Let's begin answering the first question, "When does Scripture declare that life begins?" by taking a look at one of the most well-known accounts in all of Scripture and observing how God weaves the significance of an unborn baby into it, giving us evidence that life is present at conception.

The first twenty verses of the second chapter of Luke (the narrative of the birth of Jesus) are probably some of the most well-known (and memorized) scriptures in all the world based on their repetitive recitation at numerous Christmas programs every December to what many households read every Advent season as they remember the birth of their Savior.

But if we look back at the first chapter of Luke, the precursor to the actual birth of Christ, and the events we are told about in Mary's pregnancy with Jesus, we are given a beautiful glimpse into how we know life is present at conception:

> In those days Mary arose and went with haste into the hill country, to a town in Judah, and she entered the house of Zechariah and greeted Elizabeth. And when Elizabeth heard the greeting of Mary, the baby leaped in her womb. And Elizabeth was filled with the Holy Spirit, and she exclaimed with a loud cry, "Blessed are you among women, and blessed is the fruit of your womb! And why is this granted to me that the mother of my Lord should come to me? For behold, when the sound of your greeting came to my ears, the baby in my womb leaped for

joy. And blessed is she who believed that there would be a fulfillment of what was spoken to her from the Lord." (Luke 1:39–45 ESV)

Many of you may have read these verses multiple times and are very familiar with them, but take just a moment to focus on one beautiful component weaved into this story—the fact that the very first person to recognize Jesus was a baby in his sixth month of gestation. The first person to acknowledge Jesus's existence on earth was a baby in the womb. Let's look at the backdrop of these verses to really take in this moment.

Just a few verses before this, we are told that when the angel Gabriel visits Mary (and tells her Elizabeth is in her sixth month of pregnancy [Luke 1:26, 36]), he reveals to her that she will conceive the "Son of the Most High." After she learns this, verse 39 declares that "in those days," Mary "arose and went with haste" to Judah to visit Elizabeth, meaning she got up (arose), packed up quickly, and left immediately to go to Elizabeth.

The trip from Nazareth, where Mary lived, to Judah was about eighty to one hundred miles and would have taken Mary about four to five days to complete.[1] That means that when Mary stepped foot into Elizabeth's house, her pregnancy was new, and she was perhaps only a few days along![2] Elizabeth confirms Mary's pregnancy immediately when she says, "Blessed is the fruit of your womb!" Mary hasn't even told her she is pregnant yet, but Elizabeth knows. And before Elizabeth even knows, verse 41 tells us that upon hearing Mary's greeting, "the baby leaped in her womb." John the Baptist was the first person to recognize Jesus in Mary's womb.

Here is what we learn from this passage: at the time of Mary's arrival at Elizabeth's home and being only a few days pregnant, the child inside her is the Messiah. The fact that John leaped at Jesus's presence tells us that Jesus was fully recognizable as *himself* at only a few days gestation. We cannot recognize a person if they aren't themselves. If Jesus was just merely a clump of tissue, there would be no reason for John the Baptist to leap with joy inside of Elizabeth.[3]

Scripture tells us that when Jesus came to earth to save us, he took on being fully human and experienced life exactly as human beings do (John 1:14; Phil. 2:6-7; Heb. 2:17-18). That means that he began life as a zygote and continued to develop and grow just like every other human being. And so, these verses proclaim to us that we as humans are alive, present, and fully ourselves (who God created us to be) at conception as well.

What is so beautiful to me about how God orchestrated this plan to unfold is that the very *first* message from the Messiah, and the very *first* way the Messiah makes himself known, is as an unborn baby in some of the earliest days of human life. And not only that, the first person to acknowledge and recognize the Savior of the world was *another* unborn baby. What a *powerful* statement the God of the universe proclaimed to the world that day. He proclaimed the value of life in the womb with one of the most well-known and important accounts in history, and I fully believe that one of the reasons his plan unfolded this way was because he knew of the millions of families that would be questioning the value of their babies that die before birth. He knew what their hearts would be asking and declared with the Savior of the world that a human being exists from conception.

EVIDENCE OF IDENTITY AND PERSONHOOD IN THE WOMB

That same evidence of identity or personhood in the womb is also seen in other passages throughout Scripture. In fact, there are multiple scriptures that tell us about the creation and life of a baby in the womb. Here are a few things the Bible teaches us.

God Is the One Who Forms Us in the Womb

- *Psalm 139:13–16*: "For you created my inmost being; you knit me together in my mother's womb. I praise you because I am fearfully and wonderfully made; your works are wonderful, I know that full well. My frame was not hidden from you when I was made in the secret place, when I was woven together in the depths of the earth. Your eyes saw my unformed body; all the days ordained for me were written in your book before one of them came to be."
- *Job 31:15*: "Did not he who made me in the womb make them? Did not the same one form us both within our mothers?"
- *Isaiah 44:2*: "This is what the LORD says—he who made you, who formed you from the womb..."
- *Isaiah 49:5*: "He who formed me from the womb to be his servant..."
- *Jeremiah 1:5*: "Before I formed you in the womb I knew you, before you were born I set you apart; I appointed you as a prophet to the nations."

God Declared His Purposes for His People While They Were in the Womb

- *Galatians 1:15*: "But when God, who set me apart from my mother's womb and called me by his grace, was pleased."

- *Luke 1:15*: "For he will be great in the sight of the Lord. He is never to take wine or other fermented drink, and he will be filled with the Holy Spirit even before he is born."
- *Isaiah 49:1*: "Before I was born the LORD called me; from my mother's womb he has spoken my name."
- *Genesis 25:23*: "The LORD said to her, 'Two nations are in your womb, and two peoples from within you will be separated; one people will be stronger than the other, and the older will serve the younger.'"
- *Jeremiah 1:5*: "Before I formed you in the womb I knew you, before you were born I set you apart; I appointed you as a prophet to the nations."

God Knows Us before We Are Even Formed

- *Jeremiah 1:5*: "Before I formed you in the womb I knew you, before you were born I set you apart; I appointed you as a prophet to the nations."
- *Psalm 139:16*: "Your eyes saw my unformed body; all the days ordained for me were written in your book before one of them came to be."

Each of these verses shares some incredible and rich details about life in the womb, but I want to point out in particular how personhood is made evident. The authors use the personal pronouns *I* and *me* when describing themselves in the womb. And the Lord says in Jeremiah 1:5 (NIV—emphasis mine), "Before I formed *you* in the womb I knew *you*, before *you* were born I set *you* apart; I appointed *you* as a prophet to the nations." The authors don't refer to themselves in the womb as anything except just that—themselves. If they were just merely clumps of cells, or something insignificant, then there would be no need to make it clear that they were unique, distinguished, and set apart from everyone else *before* their birth.⁴ Why mention their creation in the womb if it weren't important or worthwhile? Why not wait and declare personhood until after they were born? Psalm 139:14 specifically declares this. It says that we are "wonderfully made." The original Hebrew word for "wonderfully" is the word *pālâ*, and it means to "be distinct, marked out, separated, and distinguished." David makes known in this psalm how the Lord "knit him together in his mother's womb," and then he proclaims that he is wonderfully made, completely unique and unlike anyone else.⁵

* * *

Science has also declared that a new human life begins at the moment of conception. Leading embryologists have stated that "fertilization is a critical landmark because . . . a new, genetically distinct human organism is thereby formed."⁶ What this statement expresses to us is that a new human being that is genetically unlike any other human being that has ever existed is (by the definition of an organism) alive and growing at the moment of conception.⁷

Scientific discovery has also confirmed that *all* the genetic information needed to grow a human being is present at the moment of conception, and that genetic information is unchanging. This means that a fully grown adult contains the *exact* same genetic blueprint they had as a zygote. Nothing genetically is added or altered later.⁸

What that declares is that each of the stages of development that occur during pregnancy (zygote, embryo, and fetus) are all simply just stages of development in the life of a human being. Just as a neonate, a toddler, an adolescent, and an adult are also different stages in the life of a human being, a zygote, embryo, and fetus are merely the absolute earliest stages of development in the life of a human. And as each stage occurs (both before and after birth), a human continually grows and becomes capable of doing more. But a human's capability for what they can and cannot do does not dictate how "human" or "alive" they are. For example, we know that a toddler cannot do everything that an adolescent can, and an adolescent is not a fully developed adult either. Specific organs and certain parts of the brain have not fully developed. Just the same, a zygote cannot do everything a fetus can. But just because a human in an earlier stage of development cannot do all that another human in a later stage of development can does not make them any less alive, less human, or less themselves.[9]

In a study that surveyed over 5,500 biologists at over one thousand academic institutions, *96 percent* of the biologists agreed that because of the scientific evidence, life cannot begin at any other time than fertilization.[10] Science shows us that life begins at conception. But where there continue to be disagreements among many is the question of when significance or personhood begins, which is an issue that we have seen before in humanity.

Tragically, the world has seen systems of slavery, support for eugenics, and even genocide throughout history. Such thinking becomes possible when someone takes it upon themselves to determine another person's worth. Both the slave trade and the Holocaust are examples in history where people have acknowledged someone's humanity while simultaneously disregarding their significance, importance, or the fact that they're even a person.

This happens often with the unborn, regardless of the fact that the evidence is there. Scripture, however, discloses the answer to that question for us. It declares that life, significance, importance, and personhood all begin at the moment of conception.

Now with technology, we have been able to see something so incredible that happens at the beginning of every human life. In 2011, scientists at Northwestern University captured images of the moment that a sperm cell unites with an egg cell. What happens is remarkable. The moment the two come together, billions of zinc atoms are released, and a flash of light is emitted, radiating around the outside of the egg cell. It is breathtaking and has since been referred to by many as "the Spark of Life." In 2014, they were able to capture the phenomenon on video, and you can easily do a search online to view this for yourself.[11]

Only our God would create a radiant burst of light in a completely dark and unseen place to mark the moment a new life begins. I think immediately of all the scriptures that talk about light, especially light in the darkness. I think about the beginning when God created the heavens and the earth, how "darkness was over the face of the deep," and how the very first thing God spoke into existence was light (Gen. 1:1-3). And then I think about God's plan of redemption for all mankind, about how life comes from Christ, who declared that he is the light of the world and that our redemption comes from him alone.

> In him was life, and that life was the light of all mankind. The light shines in the darkness, and the darkness has not overcome it. (John 1:4-5)

> I am the light of the world. Whoever follows me will not walk in darkness, but will have the light of life. (John 8:12 ESV)

God is light (1 John 1:5), Christ is light (John 8:12), life comes from the Light (John 8:12), and the very first thing that occurs when a new human is conceived is a burst of light. What a magnificent Creator we have.

GOD DOES NOT DIFFERENTIATE A BABY INSIDE THE WOMB FROM A BABY OUTSIDE THE WOMB

The third thing we see in Scripture that confirms life begins at conception is that God does not differentiate a child outside of the womb from a child in the womb. We can see this by examining a few of the original Hebrew and Greek words used for babies both in the womb and outside of the womb.

For example, the word *brephos* is the Greek word that was used for John the Baptist in Elizabeth's womb in Luke 1:41 and 44 (emphasis mine): "the *baby* leaped in her womb" and "the *baby* in my womb leaped for joy."

This is also the same word used in Luke 2:12 and 16 (emphasis mine) when referring to Jesus after his birth: "you will find a *baby* wrapped in swaddling cloths" and find "Mary and Joseph and the *baby* lying in the manger."

Luke also used the same word for "infants" in Luke 18:15, when people were bringing their children to Jesus that "he might touch them" (bless them) and for "infants" in Acts 7:19. The same author used the same word in the writing of his gospel account and the book of Acts to refer to a child both inside the womb and outside the womb. Another important factor to note is that Luke was a physician (Col. 4:14), so he would have naturally paid close attention to and written his gospel and the book of Acts with incredible detail. In fact, he had other words in his vocabulary for children, yet he did not use them here. If there was a distinction between the children he was writing about, it would be easy to conclude that he would have used different words for each.

Brephos is also the word for "childhood" in 2 Timothy 3:15.

Another example of this from Scripture is the Hebrew word *ôlēl*. This is the word for "child" in 1 Samuel 15:3, and it is also the same word used for "infant" in Job 3:16 when Job is referring to the stillbirth of "an infant who never saw the light of day."

And in Genesis 25:22, Jacob and Esau are referred to as "children" while they are in Rebekah's womb.

What these comparisons show us is that God, being the authority of all Scripture, considers a baby in the womb equal to a baby outside of the womb.[12]

GOD VALUES AN UNBORN BABY'S LIFE AS MUCH AS AN ADULT'S LIFE

To answer our second question, "Does God value babies in the womb?" there is one passage in Scripture that in my opinion makes it undeniably clear that, yes, God does value babies in the womb. It also further proves life begins at conception. That passage is Exodus 21:22–25: "When men strive together and hit a pregnant woman, so that her children come out, but there is no harm, the one who hit her shall surely be fined, as the woman's husband shall impose on him, and he shall pay as the judges determine. But if there is harm, then you shall pay life for life, eye for eye, tooth for tooth, hand for hand, foot for foot, burn for burn, wound for wound, stripe for stripe."

This passage is a part of the Mosaic law, which is the law that God gave to Moses for the Israelites after their Exodus from Egypt. This law begins with the Ten Commandments and extends into every area of life, including civil and criminal matters, how to worship God, what to eat and not eat, how and when to rest, and so on.

These verses are in the midst of a series of laws about fighting and quarreling. What they say is that when a situation arises where men are fighting and a pregnant woman is accidentally hit in the midst of it, causing her to go into labor prematurely, there must be recompense. It is this recompense or compensation that shows us just how much God values the life of a baby in utero.

The Hebrew phrase in verse 22, "so that her children come out," is a combination of the noun *yeled* and the verb *yasa*, and together they mean "the child comes forth."

So in this particular scenario in these verses, there is a pregnant woman who has been hit, and as a result, her child (or children) has been born prematurely. What happens next is that a judge will evaluate the entire situation, and there are two verdicts as possibilities.

The first possible verdict is that when the woman is hit and the child comes forth but there is "no harm" to either the mother or the child, then the man who hit her must solely be fined whatever amount the woman's husband imposes and the judge sees fit.

But if the child comes forth and there "is harm" to either the mother or the child, then the compensation must be equivalent, including the consequence of "life for life."

Notice that there is no specification as to who must be harmed for the "life to life" to come into effect. This means that if the pregnant woman *or* the child that "comes forth" dies, then the man who killed either one of them should, as the judge sees fit, in return have his life taken.

For me, this couldn't be any clearer. If God requires that a man's life be taken when he accidentally takes the life of an unborn baby, then God clearly regards that unborn child's life with the same value and respect as an adult's life.

Also, notice that God does not give a specified gestational age for the unborn child. It doesn't say, "Only if a woman is over halfway through her pregnancy" or "only equal payment if a woman has felt the baby move." What a beautiful and concrete declaration that life for God begins and has the highest value from day one in the womb.[13]

SEEING OUR BABIES IN HEAVEN

Now that we have answered our two important questions and have confirmation that all babies are unique, distinct human beings at conception, and that God highly values their life inside the womb, let's look at what Scripture conveys to us about seeing our babies in heaven: "He said, 'While the child was still alive, I fasted and wept, for I said, "Who knows whether the Lord will be gracious to me, that the child may live?" But now he is dead. Why should I fast? Can I bring him back again? I shall go to him, but he will not return to me'" (2 Sam. 12:22–23).

You'll likely remember these verses from the story of David and Bathsheba that was discussed in Chapter Four. The child they conceived and bore has just died, and these two verses give us David's response to his son's death. He says, "I shall go to him, but he will not return to me."

David declares here his understanding that his son is gone and will never return to life here on earth, but he also declares with confidence that he will one day go to his son.

In Psalm 23:6, David proclaims his certainty of spending eternity in heaven when he says, "I shall dwell in the house of the Lord forever," so for David to know that he would see his child again one day tells us that his child must be in heaven, not hell.

Some people point to the fact that his child was already born when he died, so it doesn't necessarily conclude that unborn babies go to heaven when they die. But just as we saw earlier, the words used in this passage show us that God doesn't differentiate between a baby inside the womb and a baby after birth. The original Hebrew word for David's "child" in verse 22 is *yeled*. This is the *same* word used in Exodus 21:22-25 that we just discussed, referring to a child who dies while in the womb after a pregnant woman is struck during a fight.[14]

THE CHARACTER OF GOD

Lastly, I believe it's vital when answering the question "Do unborn babies go to heaven?" to examine the character of our God. The character of someone tells us who they truly are at their core, not just who they say they are or appear to be. And the Bible is the gift God gave us that gives us a glimpse into his character. It is one of the ways he reveals to us who he truly is, and he does this because he wants us to know we can trust him and that he desires a deep relationship with us. Knowing the character of God changes how we view him. It changes how we answer questions about him and questions about life. While there are multiple character attributes of God, let's look closely at just a few of them to guide us in answering our question.

God Values Human Life, Regards Children as Helpless and Vulnerable, Despises the Shedding of Their Blood, and Gives Recognition of Their Inability to Understand Good and Evil

God declares to us in Scripture how much he values human life (Gen. 9:5-6; Lev. 24:17-22). So much so that he even created a commandment stating that you shall not murder another person

(Exod. 20:13). Out of all that he created, humans are the ones who were made in God's image and likeness; we were designed to be a reflection of God himself, and we are the ones that will be coheirs with Christ after his return (Gen. 1:26–27; Rom. 8:17; Gal. 3:29).

Included in that sphere of humanity are children of all ages. There are scriptures in the Bible that address the "innocents," which are people who are considered helpless and vulnerable and cannot protect themselves from harm, danger, or starvation. Children are included in this, and God proclaims to us that we must take extra care in helping them. When people were offering their children as sacrifices, God made it very clear that that is never something he would command and that he despises the shedding of their blood (Jer. 7:31, 19:4–6).

And in Deuteronomy chapter 1, there is an "evil generation" of Israelites that God does not permit to enter the Promised Land. But the Lord does tell Moses in verse 39 that their children are allowed to enter because they "have no knowledge of good or evil" and that he will "give them the land" and "they shall possess it." The Lord conveys to us here that there is mercy given to those who don't understand the difference between good and evil.

All people inherit a sinful nature that began with Adam and Eve and is passed from one generation to the next. David declares this to us in Psalm 51:5 and states that this sinful nature is inherited at "conception." Therefore, all people, including unborn babies, need salvation in Christ.

However, because babies have not had the opportunity (nor do they have the ability) to reject God and purposefully sin against him, I believe that God will extend mercy to them, and eternal glory in heaven is theirs. This would also apply to people with mental handicaps who are also incapable of fully understanding sin and the necessary consequences of it (Rom. 1:18–32).

Jesus's Love toward Children

There are multiple verses in Scripture that reveal Jesus's deep love and compassion for children that he exhibited while he was here on earth, and as stated earlier, this includes children of all ages. In Mark 10:13–16 and Matthew 19:14 when the disciples rebuked people bringing their children to Jesus to have him bless them, Jesus was "indignant" with them and quickly corrected them, stating, "Let the little children come to me, and do not hinder them, for the kingdom of heaven belongs to such as these."

Another area in Scripture we see this is Matthew 18:1–5 (ESV): "At that time the disciples came to Jesus, saying, 'Who is the greatest in the kingdom of heaven?' And calling to him a child, he put him in the midst of them and said, 'Truly, I say to you, unless you turn and become like children, you will never enter the kingdom of heaven.'"

He Is a Loving, Merciful, and Just God

If Jesus was the *complete* image of God, then his words and actions regarding children would be a direct reflection of God the Father, meaning that from Jesus we learn that God the Father has deep compassion, love, tender affection, and respect for all children.

A Deeply Loving God

Our brains cannot even fully comprehend how vast his love is for us. It's a love so deep that he offered his own Son to die for us. And not just some of us; Christ died for all of us, because he desired nothing more than for us to spend eternity with him. Read these verses, many of which you have likely read before, and be reminded of God's immense love for his people.

- *John 3:16–17*: "For God so loved the world that he gave his only Son, that whoever believes in him should not perish but have eternal life. For God did not send his Son into the world to condemn the world, but in order the world might be saved through him."
- *Romans 5:8*: "But God shows his love for us in that while we were still sinners, Christ died for us."
- *1 John 4:7–11, 16*: "Beloved, let us love one another, for love is from God, and whoever loves has been born of God and knows God. Anyone who does not love does not know God, because God is love. In this the love of God was made manifest among us, that God sent his only Son into the world, so that we might live through him. In this is love, not that we have loved God but that he loved us and sent his Son to be the propitiation for our sins. Beloved, if God so loved us, we also ought to love one another. . . . So we have come to know and to believe the love that God has for us. God is love, and whoever abides in love abides in God, and God abides in him" (ESV).
- *1 John 3:1*: "See what great love the Father has lavished on us, that we should be called children of God! And that is what we are!"
- *Romans 8:35, 38–39*: "Who shall separate us from the love of Christ? Shall tribulation, or distress, or persecution, or famine, or nakedness, or danger, or sword? . . . For I am sure that neither death nor life, nor angels, nor rulers, nor things present nor things to come, nor powers, nor height nor depth, nor anything else in all creation, will be able to separate us from the love of God in Christ Jesus our Lord" (ESV).

A Merciful God

To show mercy, among other definitions, is to show "compassion or forbearance especially to an offender or to one subject to one's power."[15] God's mercies are "new every morning" (Lam. 3:23) for us, and because he has shown mercy by sending his Son to save us—people who have willingly sinned against him—we have every reason to believe that he would show mercy to unborn babies as well.

- *Deuteronomy 4:31*: "For the Lord your God is a merciful God; he will not abandon or destroy you or forget the covenant with your ancestors, which he confirmed to them by oath."
- *Lamentations 3:22-23*: "The steadfast love of the LORD never ceases; his mercies never come to an end; they are new every morning; great is Your faithfulness" (ESV).
- *Ephesians 2:4-5*: "But God, being rich in mercy, because of the great love with which he loved us, even when we were dead in our trespasses, made us alive together with Christ—by grace you have been saved."
- *Titus 3:4-5*: "But when the goodness and loving kindness of God our Savior appeared, he saved us, not because of works done by us in righteousness, but according to his own mercy, by the washing of regeneration and renewal of the Holy Spirit" (ESV).
- *Luke 6:36*: "Be merciful, just as your Father is merciful."
- *1 Peter 1:3*: "Blessed be the God and Father of our Lord Jesus Christ! According to his great mercy, he has caused us to be born again to a living hope through the resurrection of Jesus Christ from the dead" (ESV).

A Just God

It is impossible for God to do anything wrong. He is just and fair in all that he does, which means we can trust that in his perfect justice and love for humanity, and in his deep desire for all to be in heaven with him, he would not send children, who he views as helpless and vulnerable, to hell. We can absolutely trust that eternity in heaven is theirs.

- *Job 34:12*: "It is unthinkable that God would do wrong, that the Almighty would pervert justice."
- *Deuteronomy 32:4*: "He is the Rock, his works are perfect, and all his ways are just. A faithful God who does no wrong, upright and just is he."
- *Psalm 89:14*: "Righteousness and justice are the foundation of your throne; love and faithfulness go before you."
- *Isaiah 30:18*: "Therefore the Lord waits to be gracious to you, and therefore he exalts himself to show mercy to you. For the Lord is a God of justice; blessed are all those who wait for him" (ESV).
- *Zephaniah 3:5*: "The Lord within her is righteous; he does no injustice; every morning he shows forth his justice; each dawn he does not fail; but the unjust knows no shame" (ESV).

In summary,

God values human life.
Jesus reflected exactly who God the Father is by showing love and compassion for children while here on earth.
God sees children as helpless and vulnerable and despises the shedding of their blood.
God has an immense love for every person.

God is merciful.
God always does what is just and fair.

When we examine the character of God, every single attribute, even ones not written here, conveys to us that he is not a God who would send babies to an eternity in hell apart from him.

**

God has written Scripture exactly the way it needs to be. But many people argue that because there isn't a verse that explicitly states that "all babies that die in the womb are guaranteed salvation in heaven," that must mean where the unborn spend eternity is not significant. But I believe that God specifically did not write that one verse for a reason.

There was a pastor who gave an incredible sermon regarding the eternity of the unborn (and to this very day, I cannot find the sermon again to be able to give credit to him) where he said, "OK, let's just say, for example, that God put a verse somewhere in Scripture that said, 'Every child [which would include babies in the womb] that dies before the age of, let's say, four, is guaranteed to be in heaven with me.'"

He then said, "Let's now take that 'verse' and think about what might come of it. Can you imagine the sick cults that would form of people that would go around killing every child under the age of four, just to 'guarantee' their salvation? They would take that one verse of Scripture, twist it, and use it to justify the killing of all those children."

I then thought to myself about how that could likely include Christian parents. Most of them probably think, "Well, I don't know if my son or daughter would have rejected Christ later in his or her life, so the best thing I could do for them would be to kill them now so that their salvation would be guaranteed."

Unfortunately, this is how some people would think. In fact, even without a verse explicitly stating this, there have been people who have already done this. Andrea Yates, in 2001, drowned all five of her children because she truly believed they "would not grow up to be righteous" and that killing them before they turned sinful would save them from eternity in hell.[16]

We can truly trust that there isn't a single thing that needs to be added, rewritten, or rearranged in Scripture. We can rest in the sovereignty of God. We can rest in the fact that there are things our brains have never thought about and things outside of our control and our knowledge that we have to trust our Creator with.

We have definitively seen that the Bible is not silent on the lives of the unborn. They are no less human and no less important than a one-day-old, nine-month-old, five-year-old, teenager, or middle-aged or elderly adult. They are simply in one of the earliest stages of their lives.

This reemphasizes the heart and character of God and the answers to the questions, "Do the least of these matter? Does a person matter because of what they can do or not do?" God declares our worth is never based on what we can or cannot do. The "least of these" have always mattered to him, and he has spoken in powerful ways to show the world his love for them. As mothers who have lost babies in the earliest stages of life, we can rest in the knowledge directly from Scripture that we have the absolute joy and privilege of spending eternity with our babies in heaven.

NOTES

1. Rebecca Brant, "Explore the Life of Mary This Advent Season," Logos.com, November 16, 2012, https://www.logos.com/grow/explore-the-life-of-mary-this-advent-season/.
2. Jack Hayford, *I'll Hold You in Heaven: Healing and Hope for the Parent Who Has Lost a Child through Miscarriage, Stillbirth, Abortion, or Early Infant Death* (Minneapolis: Chosen Books, 2015), 27–32.
3. Roy B. Zuck, *Precious in His Sight: Childhood and Children in the Bible* (Eugene, OR: Wipf and Stock, 2012), 77.
4. Zuck, 77; John MacArthur, *Safe in the Arms of God: Truth from Heaven about the Death of a Child* (Nashville: Thomas Nelson, 2003), 19–22.
5. "H6395—Pālâ—Strong's Hebrew Lexicon (KJV)," Blue Letter Bible, accessed July 1, 2024, https://www.blueletterbible.org/lexicon/h6395/kjv/wlc/0-1/.
6. Ronan O'Rahilly and Fabiola Müller, *Human Embryology & Teratology* (New York: Wiley-Liss, 2001), 8, 28.
7. *Merriam-Webster*, s.v. "organism (n.)," accessed July 30, 2024, https://www.merriam-webster.com/dictionary/organism.
8. Tommy Mitchell, "When Does Life Begin?" Answers in Genesis, February 19, 2020, https://answersingenesis.org/sanctity-of-life/when-does-life-begin/.
9. Mitchell.
10. Steven Andrew Jacobs, "Balancing Abortion Rights and Fetal Rights: A Mixed Methods Mediation of the U.S. Abortion Debate" (PhD diss., University of Chicago, 2019).
11. Francesca E. Duncan et al., "The Zinc Spark Is an Inorganic Signature of Human Egg Activation," *Scientific Reports* 6, no. 24737 (2016), https://doi.org/10.1038/srep24737.
12. Zuck, *Precious in His Sight*, 76.
13. Greg Koukl, "What Exodus 21:22 Says about Abortion," Stand to Reason, February 4, 2013, https://www.str.org/w/what-exodus-21-22-says-about-abortion#.

14 "H3206—Yeled—Strong's Hebrew Lexicon (KJV)," Blue Letter Bible, accessed July 1, 2024, https://www.blueletterbible.org/lexicon/h3206/kjv/wlc/0-1/.

15 *Merriam-Webster*, s.v. "mercy (*n*.)," accessed July 1, 2024, https://www.merriam-webster.com/dictionary/mercy.

16 Marco Margaritoff, "Andrea Yates, the Texas Mom Who Drowned Her Kids to Save Them from the Devil," All That's Interesting, June 8, 2023, https://allthatsinteresting.com/andrea-yates.

CHAPTER SIX

Anguish

July 18, 2018

Soon the time came for them to take Asher away. The representative from the funeral home appeared at the door, and my heart sank knowing it was really time to say goodbye. He was so kind and gave us a few more moments to look at him and love on him before taking him away. I soaked in every second of that that I could. I looked him over up and down and made sure there was an imprint in my brain of every part of him. I held and kissed him one last time before letting the representative know he could come back in.

As he made his way through the door, I saw that he had a beautiful bassinet to place and carry him in. He took him so gently out of my hands and delicately laid him in the basket—a kindness I was grateful for. He knew that he couldn't feel any pain (as did I), but my heart absolutely could, and it was on the verge of shattering into a million pieces. For the next few minutes, he explained everything that would happen, where we needed to go, and what we needed to do to pick up his ashes. I'm grateful there were other people listening because I didn't hear a word he said. My mind blanked over, and it was all I could do to keep myself together as I prepared to watch him walk away with my son for the last time. I was fighting the voice in my head that kept telling me that if he didn't take him away, I could keep him here with me forever, simultaneously knowing that that was, of course, not possible.

He finished speaking, grabbed the bassinet, and walked toward the door. On the inside, part of me was screaming "Please don't leave. Let him stay here longer" while the other part knew this was what had to happen. I watched him walk away with our son in what seemed like slow motion (a gift from God in that moment), knowing it was the last time I would ever see Asher on this side of eternity.

Those next few moments, there was a deafening silence in that room. Understandably, no one knew what to say or do next. Really and truly, there wasn't anything you could say or do. The staff worked as hard as they could to get us out as soon as possible, knowing that we didn't want to be there any longer than we needed to.

When it was time for me to be discharged, we gathered all our things, and I was helped into a wheelchair. As soon as I sat down, my mind immediately flashed to the last two times I was in a wheelchair, holding our two other boys, and with every fiber I fought back tears. As I was wheeled out of the room, I passed by two other rooms and heard the beautiful cry of a newborn, a sound I would never hear from Asher. I just kept repeating to myself, "Just make it to the car; just make it to the car." I knew that when I got there, I could let go and let all the tears flow. Austin had pulled the car around the front of the building.

He traded places with the nurse and made his way around to the driver's side. The nurse helped me into the car, and before she could even completely shut the door, I broke. I completely collapsed and couldn't hold back the tears any longer. Every ounce of my strength was gone, and I crumbled. Austin held me for a moment and then began to drive away, and we left the hospital that day completely empty-handed.

The death of our son very forcefully reminded me of the reality of this world.

> It reminded me that we live in a world . . .
> > of sin, hurt, hardship, anguish,
> > disappointment, persecution, and death.
>
> A world . . .
> > where people go to bed hungry each night and wake up not knowing if they'll eat that day either.
> > Where men, women, and children of all ages experience physical, emotional, and sexual abuse on a daily basis.
> > Where people are treated differently, tortured, or killed because of their race, ethnicity, disability, or religion.
> > Where evil laughs in the face of good.
> > Where truth gets twisted into lies.
>
> A world . . .
> > of constant bullying.
> > Where sickness and disease change the course of people's lives, if not taking them completely.

Where death, even death seemingly way too soon, is an absolute certainty.
A world where, in a lot of ways, *suffering seems to reign*.

And there's not a single person who's exempt from it. We are absolutely guaranteed to walk through hardship in our lives. And while some trials are bearable, others threaten to steal life out of us. They make our legs unable to hold us up, they take the breath out of our lungs in an instant, and they make us not want to go on living another day.

While my face was abruptly turned to see and experience one of the realities of suffering in this world, God has also gently taken my head in his hands and turned my gaze back on him. He has taught me what it means to suffer. That there *is* meaning to it, and that one day it will be gone forever. As Elisabeth Elliot so beautifully said, "Suffering is never for nothing."[1]

But one of the hardest things to grapple with is why God *allows* such immense suffering in our lives. Because that is the truth: God is sovereign over all of it. And if we know and truly believe what Scripture says, that God is in control of every second of every day, then that means that God *does allow*, and even causes, the suffering in our lives. That means that he can prevent or stop suffering at any point, yet there are moments where he doesn't.

Why?

Why does a good God allow the people that he loves to suffer such substantial anguish? Why would he allow and cause trials that seemingly break us? Why would he take away the lives of people we love long before they have even "lived"?

Suffering in our lives makes us question the goodness and love of our God. It causes us to wrestle with things we've always believed and known about him that are now put to the test. We question the certainty of the character traits of God that are true of him.

> Is he really loving? Merciful? Good? Just?
> Righteous in all that he does?
>
> If he is, then how can he allow such unbearable things to happen to us?

When we are plummeted into deep valleys because of tragedy in our lives, our faith is put under fire. The foundation of my faith going into the valley that I had now been asked to walk through was, by God's grace, sturdy. And deep within me, I knew with certainty that God was good no matter what happened. But after Asher's death, I found myself at a crossroads of truth and reality, and that faith was put to the test. In one hand, I held the definitive truth from Scripture that God is completely sovereign and can *only* do good, but in the other hand, I held the reality of death and suffering in the world. And although in that moment my heart and mind were mostly focused on what was in the second hand, God reminded me that I must also take into consideration the verity that was held in the first hand.

So while my lament at the start of that crossroads continually revolved around the question "Why, Lord? Why would you allow this?" it then, because of God's gentle reminder, shifted to "Help me to understand."

One of the first things God taught me about enduring tragedy is that we are not going to know every reason behind our suffering. Even though God is deeply concerned with each and every one of us, he does not always give us the answers we want to our most agonizing questions. And sometimes this causes us to dance back and forth with God. One minute we are close to him, resting and trusting in all that we know about him, and the next we are across the dance floor, seeing him from a distance and wondering if we can trust him (because he hasn't given us exactly what we desire) as we carry on.

An example of this in Scripture is found at the end of the book of Lamentations. Lamentations is a memorial to the pain and confusion of the Israelites following the Babylonian siege and the complete destruction of Jerusalem. And through five different poems of lament, it articulates the many faces of grief felt by the Israelites during that time.

The author begins the book by relaying to God the horrible things that happen in this world that should not be tolerated. The lament is then used as a way to process emotion where God's people vent their anger and dismay at people's selfishness. And lastly, the book is used as a place to voice confusion to God about suffering and about his character. All these things—anger, dismay, confusion about suffering, questioning God's character, processing emotion—are likely what we as mothers who have lost babies have felt.

The ending, however, is a beautiful example of what some of our conversations and laments with God sound like after tragedy. It pinballs back and forth between the truth of God and the reality of this world. It begins by first acknowledging that God does and will reign forever over all generations but then says, "Why do you forget us forever, why do you forsake us for so many days?" (Lam. 5:19-20 ESV).

The author then professes God's authority by asking him to "restore" them as a people back to him and to "renew our days of old," but the author ends the book by saying, "unless you have utterly rejected us, and you remain exceedingly angry with us" (Lam. 5:21-22 ESV).

It's a conclusion that doesn't give us closure or a black-and-white "answer," exactly like so many of our own experiences of pain and suffering. They don't always have neat, tidy endings, and there are days when we feel like our emotions are bouncing back and forth between the truth of God and the reality of a fallen world.

We see this in the book of Job as well. Tragedy strikes, and Job displays remarkable faith through his affliction, but he also questions God's ways: "Though he slay me, yet will I hope in him; I will surely defend my ways to his face" (Job 13:15).

But what both of these books show us is that God purposefully and intentionally gives voice to the suffering. He is not asking anyone to suffer in silence or deny their emotions but to voice their protest and pour out their feelings before God.

We might not always have the exact answer or reason as to why tragedies occur in our lives, but we do not have to. Because God is all-knowing, we don't have to know everything. Because God sees everything, we don't need to. Because he is always working, we can rest in him.

All we need to do is trust him.

Although we do not know the ways of God because his ways are infinitely higher than our own (Isa. 55:9), we do get the privilege of watching God take the tragedies in our lives, bring glory from them, and use them to grow the Kingdom. Let's look at some of the ways he does this.

OUR CONSTANT REMINDER

One very prominent reason God allows suffering is humans need to be reminded of sin in the world and our need for a Savior. I think it's easy to go through the motions of everyday things and settle into normal rhythms and comforts and forget about the reality that this life ends and eternity follows after it.

And particularly, when people hear about and experience the suffering that comes with the death of someone they love, it causes them to pause in their tracks and reminds them that every day is not guaranteed. Deaths in our lives, especially the deaths of little ones, force us to think about heaven and to grab hold of each and every day as if it were our last; death is our reminder that we must make every day a fight for the Kingdom.

There is an urgency to put aside small talk about meaningless things because the reality of this life is now at the forefront of our minds. Instead of spending conversations talking about things that don't matter and fade away, we take the time to ask real questions and bring up the hard topics that need to be spoken about to bring healing, restoration, and the verity of the gospel.

God uses suffering to remind us of our reality: we live in a world with death woven in its fibers and a blatant need for the Savior.

A WITNESS TO THOSE WHO DON'T KNOW CHRIST

For people who don't know Jesus, one of the most powerful witnesses is suffering within the life of a believer. Because when others can see the faith we talk so much about and our belief and understanding of our God put firmly to the test, then there is validation that what we have been telling them is true.

When all that we claim is put directly into the flames, and we walk out of the furnace with an understanding and faith that is even greater than it was before, *that's* when others want to know what it is we have. *That's* when others want to know who God is and how in the world we can look suffering and tragedy directly in the eye and shout even louder than before that our God is good.

Think of it this way: if our lives as believers were exempt from any type of tragedy, it would be easy for those who don't know Christ to question the reality and love of God.

It would be easy for others to look at our seemingly perfect lives and say, "Well of course you believe in a loving God because you haven't had to endure what I have. You've never had to experience true hunger or not knowing if your lights are going to turn on when you flip the switch. You've never watched your sister die an excruciating death from cancer or gotten a phone call that your mother was hit by a drunk driver while walking home. You've never lived with chronic pain or disease that limits what you can experience or do in this life. Of course you can believe in a 'good' God because you've never had to experience anything that isn't good."

Satan proposes this same thing at the beginning of the book of Job. He says to God, "Does Job fear God for no reason? Have you not put a hedge around him and his house and all that he has, on every side? You have blessed the work of his hands, and his possessions have increased in the land. But stretch out your hand and touch all that he has, and he will curse you to your face" (Job 1:9-11).

Satan is saying that the only reason Job honored and feared God the way he did was because he had no reason to hate him. Job was wealthy and prosperous, and God was protecting him on all sides. So Satan challenged God to take all of it away, fully believing that Job would then curse God to his face, yet he never did.

It's hard when you've suffered immense hardship to want to believe that there is a God who is supposed to be good and loving but is seemingly just "sitting up in heaven" allowing all this to unfold here on earth.

But that is one of the reasons God allows suffering in our lives. When other people who don't know the truth of the gospel can look into our lives as believers and see that even in the middle of a hurricane we have peace and are still giving praise and glory to God, they will absolutely ask, "Why?" Because it doesn't make sense. They will want to know the reason why we can still call God good and have joy and hope in the middle of tragedy.

Why, after everything that Job went through, did he still call God good? Why, after losing his children and property, cursing the day of his birth, and wishing he was dead, was he still praising the God in control of all of it? Why was Paul able to sit on the floor of a prison cell after being brutally beaten and still write Ephesians, Philippians, Colossians, and Philemon?

Because they always held fast to whose child they were: children of the living God. And they knew that no matter what happened to them in this life, God is still who he says he is. And that's what we must remember too.

When we let the truth of God and the gospel lead our hearts and lives, that's when others can see the light of Christ beaming through us, even in the deepest and darkest moments of life, where we need light the most. When we can look death straight in the eye and say, "Where is your victory and your sting?" (1 Cor. 15:55), that's when others will say, "Help me to understand."

A LIGHT FOR THOSE WHO DO KNOW CHRIST

Each of us as believers holds the truth of God (who he is and what he's promised) and the gospel in our hands. We hold the good news that our Savior came and died for all, and now sin and death have been defeated, and freedom, abundant life, and glory are ours for eternity. We have the Spirit of the Living God within us, and therefore that truth is deeply known and understood, and it is ours to take hold of and live by.

But in the midst of tragedy, we are faced with a choice of what we will do with that truth. Will we stand there frozen with it in our hands, too afraid to take the next step forward? Will we put it down at our sides or possibly even behind our backs, forgetting or pretending like it doesn't exist? Or will we take that truth, move it close to our hearts, and begin walking forward, letting it lead the way?

What God reminded me through Asher's death is that when we watch other believers put the gospel into action and walk through this life letting it lead the way, it inspires others and reminds them of all that Christ died for. Freedom and abounding life are not just for eternity; they are for our lives right now.

Paul reminds us in 1 Thessalonians 4:13 that our grief should not look the same as those who have no hope. The loss of the people we love—the loss of our babies, for us—is not hopeless. Is it painful? Yes. But we know this is not the end because Christ defeated death, and therefore, we have the absolute privilege and joy to spend our lives knowing and living the glory that is ours. We get the joy of waking up every day knowing we will see our children again. That is our truth and freedom that we get to cling to and walk forward with.

We also have the Spirit of the Living God within us. The same Spirit that raised Jesus from the dead lives within you and me. That changes everything about our lives. The Holy Spirit gives us supernatural strength, peace, and comfort that we would never be able to have on our own.

In the depths of my grief, when I felt like I couldn't even lift my head off the pillow much less muster up the strength needed to move forward, I *needed* to see other believers living out their faith. I needed to see that there was a light at the end of the tunnel and that this pain would not last forever. I needed to know that someone else had been in my shoes with wavering hope but clung to the truth and the promises of God and made it through.

And now we get to do that for others who are walking the same trials we are. We get to be part of the evidence that God is faithful and always near to the brokenhearted and that even in some of the most heartbreaking moments here on earth, we can declare that God is still who he says he is and healing is possible.

A MEANS TO GROW US

Many of the stories that I have heard and read talk about how the hardest and most challenging moments in someone's life were the ones where God grew them the most. They were the moments where character was challenged and developed and bravery and strength now prevailed. They were moments where immaturity was made into maturity and faith was anchored deeper than before.

Most people when they think about blessings from God think about prosperity, good health, and so on. But oftentimes, suffering is where God actually blesses us the most. It's hard to think of suffering in our lives as a blessing. But our trials put us in a posture that allows God to give us things far better than any amount of money, job, or person could ever give us.

And for many people, their trials were places they felt the closest to God. Their suffering caused them to shut out everything in the world and grow their relationship with Christ deeper than they could have ever imagined. If suffering is inevitable in our lives, and God of course knows this, then it begs us to recognize how deep the kindness of God is—that he would take the worst moments of our lives and build good from them.

He uses them to continually shape us to be more like Christ and prepare us for the inheritance that is ours.

WORSHIP AMID SUFFERING

I love meeting people and reading stories about those who have endured unbearable heartbreak yet instinctively dropped to their knees and worshiped God right in the middle of the storm. For them, worship in tragedy has become a reflex. The weight of adversity hits them, and they know the only person they can turn to and the only place they need to be is in the presence of the Lord.

For others, it's not necessarily an immediate response but a developing one. There is wondering and questioning and pleading before being moved to a place of worship.

I find it so interesting and fitting that when tragedy strikes our lives, the first body parts that become weak are our knees and legs. We drop to the floor and can no longer take steps forward in the direction we are going. And we are automatically and immediately in a posture to not only pray but also worship.

The purpose of worship is to create an intimate space between you and the Lord, allowing him to speak directly to your heart so that you are drawn nearer to him. Not only that, but it also creates a protective wall around your heart to combat spiritual warfare. I can absolutely guarantee that in the throes of suffering and when tragedy strikes, the enemy will put in overtime to try to convince you that God is not good and that you therefore have no reason to trust him. Every flaming arrow will be launched your way. But worship is a way to quiet the enemy and the rest of the world and focus your mind on God.

Job does it immediately after finding out his children have died and his property has been taken: "Then Job arose and tore his robe and shaved his head and fell on the ground and worshiped. And he said, 'Naked I came from my mother's womb, and naked shall I return. The LORD gave and the LORD has taken away; blessed be the name of the LORD'" (Job 1:20–21 ESV).

And you'll recall that David did the same after the death of his first son: "And David said to his servants, 'Is the child dead?' They said, 'He is dead.' Then David arose from the earth and washed and anointed himself and changed his clothes. And he went into the house of the LORD and worshiped" (2 Sam. 12:19–20 ESV).

The writer of the book of Hebrews shares with us an image of gathered worship that has deepened my understanding of the magnitude of it and has brought me so much comfort after losing Asher. The author is writing to believers who likely will or have altogether given up meeting in community with each other and are regressing in their faith. These verses were written to encourage those believers by revealing to them what happens when we gather together in assembled worship and enter into the presence of God. The writer says,

> But you have come to Mount Zion and to the city of the living God, the heavenly Jerusalem, and to innumerable angels in festal gathering, and to the assembly of the firstborn who are enrolled in heaven, and to God, the judge of all, and to the spirits of the righteous made perfect, and to Jesus, the mediator of a new covenant, and to the sprinkled blood that speaks a better word than the blood of Abel. (Heb. 12:22–24 ESV)

The author has painted this beautiful picture for us of what occurs when we as an "assembly" of believers come before the throne of God in heaven (Mount Zion), the heavenly Jerusalem, and Jesus (who sits at the right hand of God) in worship. The writer declares that as we worship, we participate with countless angels, the assembly of the firstborn whose names have been written in the Book of Life, and the spirits of the righteous made perfect. The spirits of the righteous are the saints of the old and new covenants who have died and are now in heaven in God's presence, made holy and perfect. This includes our ancestors and our loved ones who have gone before us in Christ. And this includes our babies who are also now in glory.

When we gather to worship our God, we are joining our sons and daughters who are also before the throne, lifting up and praising our God and Savior. We are joining our parents and siblings if they have already been called home, and our grandparents, great-grandparents, great-great-grandparents, and so on. We are joining the Hall of Faith: Abel, Enoch, Noah, Abraham, Sarah, Issac, Jacob, Joseph, Moses, and Rahab. And we are joining Peter, Paul, Mary, Anna, Phoebe, and so many other heroes of the faith.

Now when I worship with the saints here on earth, I don't want to miss a single day of it because I know that we are joining that great assembly in heaven, including my son, all standing, kneeling, bowing, dancing, and congregating before the throne.

***

When you examine the stories in Scripture of people who have suffered specifically related to the loss of a child, there is a multitude of names we do not know, like the names of the parents who lost their sons as a result of Herod's rage and subsequent slaughter of every male child age two and under (Matt. 2:16), but there are also some you are likely familiar with:

Adam and Eve, Judah, Aaron, Rachel, Rizpah, David and Bathsheba, Job, and Mary (Jesus's mother).

There are also many accounts of women who struggled with infertility:

Sarah, Rebekah, Rachel, and Hannah.

And although Scripture does not specifically say these women lost babies during pregnancy, it could be possible that loss was a part of their story as well.

But Mary's story in particular speaks loudly to the hurting hearts of mothers who have lost children. When we reflect on her life, from being chosen by God to raise the Messiah to then watching him die an excruciating death, we can cling to the fact that an ordinary woman was appointed by God to walk through something both beautiful and excruciatingly hard.

She was blessed with the life of her son and the privilege of raising the Son of God, but she also had to stand by while he was persecuted, tortured, and eventually killed on the cross. Yes, she knew Jesus was the Son of God, but he was also her son. She carried him in pregnancy, gave birth to him, taught him to walk and talk, fed him, played with him, sang to him, and told him stories. She comforted him when he was hurt and showed him all the things every mother shows her children. And then when it was time for him to step into ministry, she surrendered her son to the Lord. Although she knew and trusted in all that God had planned for her son, I can only imagine the thoughts and questions that ran through her head as she watched each step of the plan unfold.

While our stories do look very different from hers, we can look at what a beautiful example of surrender her life is for us.

We can look at how she surrendered not only her life, and all the plans she had for it, but also her son's life and the dreams she had for him as well.

It's an incredibly hard thing to do. Seemingly impossible at times. But the moment we hand it all over to him—our children's lives, our own lives, our husband's lives, our careers, our money, our strengths, our weaknesses, our houses, our material things, our sufferings—is the moment we experience the freedom that Christ died for. It's the moment we get to say,

> "Even if I lose it all, I know that my Redeemer lives, and all is not lost."

It's the moment we are reminded that in Christ we are made whole, even when parts of us are missing. Because of his death and resurrection, those holes in our bodies, from the pieces that are gone now or from the wounds we have obtained, are completely filled. There may be scars and aches that are temporary, but because of him, each and every one of us has been made whole. We get to walk in celebration knowing that those pieces of us that are gone have already been restored and in perfection are awaiting us in heaven.

And while we wait here on earth, we have the choice to look at suffering through a different lens. We can see it as an end, or we can look at all that God calls us to walk through as an opportunity for glory. We suffer for Christ just as he suffered for us.

When we look at the life of our Savior and truly reflect on the substantial anguish he endured while he was here, we can begin to look at the suffering in our own lives a little differently. We can't fully comprehend all that Christ had to bear while he was here, but what we can understand is that he endured every moment of that suffering for *us*. His life was not a "normal," constantly happy, comfortable life. There was immense loss, heartache, grief, persecution, physical agony, and eventual death. And every bit of it was for us.

And so, when I look at my own life and the hard trials the Lord has called me to walk through, I can stand proudly in the shoes he has placed my feet in because of just that: the knowledge and understanding that the God of the universe is the one who placed me there. He chose me to walk through the specific trial of losing a baby just as he has asked others to walk through the same thing or other tragedies.

I can look at all of it, even the suffering, as a privilege. I can look those adversities directly in the eye and rest in the fact that they do not last forever, even if the wounds from them last the rest of this life here on earth. I can look death in the eye and proclaim that Jesus has already defeated it. After this life, death will be no more. I can rest in the fact that my son is in heaven, dwelling in the presence of Jesus and experiencing more joy than he could have ever experienced here on earth. And one day, I get to experience that indescribable joy with him.

NOTE

1 Elisabeth Elliot, *Suffering Is Never for Nothing* (Brentwood, TN: B & H, 2019).

CHAPTER SEVEN

Graves into Gardens

August 21, 2018

Look at all these beautiful dahlias. They are thriving in the garden we planted when you were alive. They bring my heart so much joy and make me think of you every time I look at them. The deepest burgundy red and the purest stark white petals. The colors of the gospel.

My heart for nature and the beauty it brings has changed and grown so much since you left. I see God more vividly in all of it than I ever have before. He is speaking to me through it. In everything I look at now—whether it's the clouds, flowers, trees, a sunset, or even feeling the wind—all I see is heaven. I see God and his mercy and am reminded that he is always here with us. No matter how many times my feelings make me think he isn't near, he is. He never leaves us. He uses the world to speak to us and to show us who he is. To show us his beauty and his goodness in the times and places when darkness seems to prevail.

My pregnancy with Asher was by far my hardest. I had morning sickness with both Liam and Graham that, like clockwork, started at week six and lasted until week sixteen and was not simply "morning" sickness but "all-day" sickness. And so, when I started getting waves of nausea at week four with Asher, I knew this pregnancy was not going to be any different. But this time, it was far more intense. I spent many hours a day next to the toilet or on the couch trying to recover. I had a three-year-old and a one-year-old at the time, and between the sickness and keeping up with all of life, I was wiped out.

But it was springtime, and I was determined to get some flowers planted in the ground. That winter, I had chosen a small section of our yard to turn into a flower garden and got a few of the first flowers planted that spring. After long days where I had two little ones attached to my hip, I would take some time in the evening after Austin got home from work to go outside and work as much as I could in this garden. That garden ended up being one of the only things that Asher and I did together just the two of us. But the only flowers that ended up blooming later that summer were the dahlias. I hadn't noticed at the time of choosing, but the two colors I planted were deep burgundy red and bright, pure white.

The colors of the gospel.

And for many weeks after we lost him, I would go out and cut flowers and spend time in that garden because it was a delicate place filled with his memory. A place that was for just him and me. I hadn't realized the specific colors of the flowers at first until a friend wrote me the most heartfelt letter after sharing a picture of the dahlias on social media. She pointed out that it was no coincidence that the colors representing Christ's death and resurrection were the only ones that bloomed. And God, knowing and orchestrating all things, arranged this letter and realization at the best time because in the throes of my grief, I had been questioning whether Asher was in heaven and if I would ever get to see him again. It was as if, in that moment, the Lord gently whispered,

> "Remember who I died for."

I ended up dedicating that garden to him, naming it Asher's Garden. It has been filled with many other flowers, and I will continue adding more each year.

Planting a garden is just one of the many, many ways you can celebrate, remember, and cherish the life of your baby. There are so many beautiful and uniquely personal ways for you to not only express grief but also honor your son or daughter's life. Here are a few others.

NAME YOUR BABY

If you haven't already, pray over a meaningful name for your baby. When Asher died, Austin and I didn't have a boy name chosen yet. One day when Austin was driving home from work, he heard the name Asher on the radio, and it resonated with him. He had been thinking about names and had liked the name James as well. He called me and asked what I thought about the name Asher James. I immediately looked up the meaning of it. *Asher* means "one who is blessed," and *James* means "happy." I immediately said, "Yes." I thought to myself, "Happy and blessed. Perfect for a baby where the first thing his eyes ever saw was the face of Jesus." His name was settled. Let the name you choose have meaning and significance.

PLANT A GARDEN OR A TREE

After we received Asher's ashes from the funeral home, Austin and I decided to have a small memorial service in our backyard. We had our parents and our pastor come to our house and chose a place to plant a tree in his memory. We incorporated some of his ashes in the dirt at the base of the tree, and our pastor shared some beautiful and comforting words with us as we continued to say goodbye to our son. Over the years, we have watched that tree grow, just as we would have watched Asher grow, and it has served as a beautiful memorial.

Planting a tree, a specific plant, or even an entire garden is a beautiful way to honor your son or daughter. We ended up doing both (you certainly don't need to do both if you don't want to). Having something in their memory that shows life is a beautiful reminder of the life they lived here on earth and the life they have now because of their Savior. Choose a tree or flowers or plants that are meaningful to you.

HANG AN ORNAMENT

I had friends who gifted us with the most thoughtful ornaments for our Christmas tree. And each year it is such a blessing to pull out those ornaments and hang them. Holidays can be very hard after losing a baby, especially Christmas. I can't help every year, when I am hanging stockings and putting up decorations, thinking about how I should be hanging up one more stocking or buying one more set of Christmas pajamas. The ache sets in a little heavier that time of year. Having a very personal ornament is a wonderful way to remember and incorporate your baby at Christmas.

MAKE A SHADOW OR KEEPSAKE BOX

There aren't many things that we have from our babies after pregnancy loss, but using shadow boxes is a great way to collectively display what we do have. You can take things like your sonogram pictures, their baby blankets, a onesie they would have worn, bows or socks, cards people sent you, anything you obtained from the hospital, a picture of your pregnancy announcement, and so on and arrange it all in a shadow box case. Or, if you prefer not to display those items, you can construct a keepsake box where you simply gather those items together, put them into a decorated box, and keep them where you prefer. You can then pull that box down and look through the items anytime you wish.

HAVE JEWELRY MADE

There are so many wonderful companies that make all kinds of jewelry that can honor your baby. There are necklaces that can be made from their ashes, your breastmilk if you had some, or even pictures that you have of them. There are bracelets, earrings, rings, anklets, and so on that can be ways to carry your son or daughter with you all the time and can even be good conversation starters. You can design any piece of jewelry to include their name, initials, birth flower or birth stone, or anything symbolic that represents them.

HANG ARTWORK

There are all kinds of incredible artists who make beautiful works to represent people's lives after they have left this earth. And hanging a piece of art on your wall is a simple but beautiful way to cherish your baby. There are artists who can create a painting from your sonogram picture. Or, if you don't have a sonogram picture, you can have a painting of your baby's birth flower made. I've also seen artwork where an artist paints a picture of your entire family and adds in a lightly shaded girl or boy to represent the baby that would have been right there next to the rest of your family. You can also frame a poem or Scripture verse that you chose for your baby.

I have listed a gift guide in the back of this book that provides a list of companies that make pieces of jewelry, art, or other gifts for grieving mothers.

CELEBRATE THEIR BIRTHDAY EACH YEAR

This should be very personal and designed however you would like. If you have other children and would like them to celebrate, something like baking a cake is a great way to involve them. Or you can simply light a candle on their birthday in honor and remembrance of them.

There is absolutely no pressure for you to do anything at all. Do not feel any guilt if you do not want to plant a garden or wear a piece of jewelry or celebrate their birthday each year. Your grief is your own, and you can express the love that you have for your child in whatever way you feel comfortable. But if you are searching for ways to express what your heart has been holding within or are looking for a physical reminder to see often, consider some of these options, and ask the Lord to show you what may be helpful and healing.

* * *

Our trials forever mark us. We are different now. And there is no going back to the way our lives were before. We cannot bring our babies back. But we can absolutely take steps forward again and continue running our race that the Lord has called us to.

I hope that after reading this, you have felt the loving arms of the Savior, give you peace and comfort.

I hope you know that you should never be ashamed to grieve the loss of your baby. And that it is not only OK but important that you grieve them. I hope you understand there is no timeline or one "right" way to grieve and that grieving is uniquely personal. I hope you can rest in the fact that we as humans were created with emotions, and therefore, expressing those emotions is what we are designed to do. I hope you know you can take every emotion and feeling and unload them before the Father; he is never surprised, angry, or upset by them. I hope you can rest in the knowledge that Jesus grieved while he was here on earth and therefore knows your pain and can grieve right alongside you.

I hope you understand that we live in a world that has no idea how to grieve this type of loss. It has been hidden for so long that many people have no clue how to respond to someone who tells them their baby has died. And while there are some people who will say hurtful statements purposefully, many have no idea that what they've said is producing more harm than good. But we have a choice as to how we respond. We have Scripture as our focal point for all that we hear, and we can always refer back to it. And God will provide opportunities to gently share the truth and help others understand the pain that can come with this type of loss.

I hope you have found comfort in understanding that your husband's grief is going to look different from yours—that he was created and designed differently than you, and therefore he is going to express his grief differently as well. I hope you understand that just because there might be a lack of tears or less verbal expression, it does not mean there is a lack of pain or caring. I hope you know that your marriage can stay anchored with Christ in the middle and strengthen exponentially as you endure this storm. There will be moments that are very hard, but those hard moments don't have to define your marriage.

I hope you know that your baby (or babies) is infinitely loved by God, and when Scripture says that Jesus died for *all*, that includes you and your babies.

I hope you can rest in the knowledge that your baby is safe in the arms of God and experiencing pure joy in heaven. I hope you have peace knowing they never had to experience the pain of this earth. They never had to experience heartbreak, possibly physical pain, sickness, disease (although some will have experienced these), bullying, or any of the effects of a world interlaced with sin. The first thing their eyes ever saw was the face of Jesus.

I hope you know that your suffering is not in vain, that God takes the absolute worst moments of life and brings beauty from the ashes of them. He does not allow tremendously hard things to take place in our lives because he does not care or because he's not paying attention. Sometimes we will get answers here on earth, and sometimes we won't. But no matter what, we have a God who is good in the times that are joyful *and* in the moments that are not.

A question I've been asked often after losing Asher is

"Do you fear death more or less now?"

My answer varied for a while. Immediately after losing him, I was certain that everyone else in my life was going to die too. Austin was going to die, and then Liam and Graham, and I needed to prepare myself to lose them as well. But then things shifted, and I felt a peace about his death and about death in general. I fully settled into a place of understanding that my son was *safe*. The fact that I never have to worry about anything bad happening to him at all resonated with me. He will never feel pain, no one will ever harm him, and he will never experience disappointment or heartache. The realization hit me that I have nothing at all to fear for him. What a gift that is to a mother's heart.

But then, I had a series of scary moments happen that really put that peace to the test. One month after Asher's death, my father had a ministroke, then about three weeks after that, the airplane Austin was on went through a massive storm that led to some very scary moments. Then about two months after that, my grandmother had a stroke and another plane Austin was on went through an extremely scary moment, both around the exact same time. I paused after all four of those events and thanked God profusely for his very evident provision in each one of those moments, but I also very bluntly asked him, "What in the world is going on, because I don't know that my heart can take much more right now?" And in that moment, he helped me once again put all of it into perspective. He again blessed me with the peace that only he can give—the same peace he surrounded our hospital room with the day we delivered Asher. And I experienced confirmation that He continually stays near to us and meets our needs exactly where they are.

Even if all those moments ended with the worst possible outcome, each of those people would have been safe. They would have been home, in heaven. Those moments helped the overwhelming fear slowly dissipate because they gave me the opportunity to cling closer to the Father and fix my eyes on heaven. By no means did that completely eradicate all fear forever and ever. There are absolutely moments when fear creeps in, and I know it always will. But I have full confidence now that the Lord meets each one of us in those instances and provides us with all we need.

* * *

One of the most comforting things I learned after Asher passed is about a phenomenon called fetal microchimerism (FMc). Mothers throughout time have instinctively known that they are deeply and intimately connected with their children. Even after they have grown and no longer need us the way they did when they were young, we still feel like we carry a piece of them with us always. Now science has told us that that's not just a feeling; it's given us proof of that truth through the study of FMc.

Microchimerism is a two-way exchange of fetal and maternal cells during pregnancy. This means that fetal cells make their way across the placenta and into the mother's bloodstream and vice versa (a mother's cells make their way into the baby's bloodstream). This exchange happens as soon as the placenta implants into the uterus (which can occur as early as six days from conception) and still happens even if the pregnancy doesn't end in a live birth. And what scientists have found is that these cells stay in our bodies for decades, and very likely the rest of our lives. That means at this moment right now, you have living cells from every one of your children within you, even your baby (or babies) that are no longer here.

It gets even more exciting.

As scientists have studied fetal microchimerism specifically, what they have found is truly remarkable. These fetal cells that have made their way into the mother's bloodstream circulate throughout the body and end up in varying tissues over time.

Some might end up in the brain, some in the heart, the kidneys, the lungs, and so on. But one of the factors that can determine where the cells land is illness or injury in the mother. Studies have shown that if the mother becomes ill or has damage to a certain place or organ within her body, groups of fetal cells rush to the site, repair it, and stay there forever. Our babies literally heal our broken bodies, and they become a part of every fiber of our being. Even if they are no longer here, you will have a part of them within you for the rest of your life.

There are many scientists who don't know how to describe it. Some have said statements like "It does seem kind of magical. Almost like science fiction, too."[1] The truth is we know that it's not magic. It's not science fiction, and it's not unexplainable. It's the perfect and intentional design of our Creator. In my years of studying the human body for nursing school, I learned so much that deepened my faith tremendously. For me, you cannot look at the human body and tell me there is no God. The complexity of it and the way that each body part works together are truly miraculous. There is absolutely no possible way that it all happened by chance. Our bodies were designed by an intelligent Creator. There is no other explanation. And knowing yet another extraordinary feature of the way God designed human bodies to work brings a smile to my face once again.

FMc is many things, but perhaps most of all, it's a gift from a Father who loves us—a Father who empathizes with our pain, meets us in it, and does not leave us. We cannot be with our children just yet. We must wait for heaven for that. But we can take great comfort in knowing that while we wait, we carry a piece of them within us.

* * *

Oftentimes, the scars we possess because of the deep wounds we have received are seen by the world as something to be covered. But I believe God looks at them differently. After all, Jesus himself, even in his perfect resurrected body, kept the scars on his hands and side from his crucifixion. In fact, the very first thing Jesus showed his disciples after his resurrection were his scars (John 20:19-20).

Our scars from our suffering are our reminders of the battles and fires we have been called to walk through. They both tell our stories to others and are reminders to us of what the Lord has sustained and carried us through.

Some of those scars are external, visible for people to be able to inquire and ask questions about. Some scars, though, are internal. They are woven into the deepest parts of us and only become visible to those who take the time to get to know us. Our Father, however, knows every single one of our scars, both the internal and the external ones, and he sees them as something beautiful.

Seeing the scars that others carry, and hearing their stories, instills in us a drive to be able to carry on. It fills us with hope that we will be able to make it through whatever hardship we are in the midst of, and it pushes us to be able to put one foot in front of the other and continue running our race until we make it Home.

When you are ready, share your scar with those who you feel need it. Part of the beauty that comes from the loss of our babies is that we now have an immediate platform to share the truth of the gospel.

If we are able to take our pain and anguish and learn how to deal well with it, we are in turn able to help others. If we are able to grab hold of our identity in Christ and the truth of the gospel, we will be able to comfort other mothers who are walking through exactly what we've walked through. And because of our firsthand experience, because we know the pain they are likely feeling, we are capable of loving them well.

Though each of our stories is unique, we do have one thing in common: our babies are gone. We cannot bring them back, we cannot hug or hold them, and we don't get to watch them grow or raise them here on earth; it's heartbreaking. But I've taken comfort in the fact that we do not have to walk through our pain alone. Our God specifically designed us to be in community together and not live in isolation, especially as we walk through the hardest moments of life.

You now carry a scar that only certain people in the world carry. A scar that will remain with you for the rest of your life and is not outwardly seen by others. It has to be unveiled in order for others to see it. I'm sorry that it's one you are called to harbor, but I'm grateful to have runners next to me as we finish the race of this life who bear the same mark I do. I had a friend who lost her son minutes after he was born tell me after we lost Asher that the rest of our lives here on earth are "only a teardrop in an ocean compared to the eternity that we will spend in heaven with them."

I know what it is to truly long for heaven now and to live knowing this is not our home. I have felt and seen the nearness of God in the darkest of moments, and I can truly say that he is a good and loving God through all of it. And I know without a doubt that because of Christ's death and resurrection on the cross, he has taken all babies, including my son, to be with him in heaven. And one day I will get to see Asher again, face-to-face, and will never have to let him go.

I can't wait.

NOTE

1 This was said by Athena Aktipis, associate professor of psychology at Arizona State University, who coauthored a study on fetal microchimerism and maternal health. Amy M. Boddy et al., "Fetal Microchimerism and Maternal Health: A Review and Evolutionary Analysis of Cooperation and Conflict beyond the Womb," *BioEssays* 37, no. 10 (August 28, 2015): 1106–18, https://doi.org/10.1002/bies.201500059, quoted in Rosie Colosi, "Mothers Always Felt like They Carried Their Children in Their Hearts Forever. Now Science Says It's True," TODAY, February 14, 2024, https://www.today.com/parents/pregnancy/microchimerism-pregnancy-loss-miscarriage-rcna138131.

BONUS CHAPTER

For Dads

Written by Austin Dickey

By no means am I a writer of any kind. So when my wife came to me and asked me to help write a chapter for her book, I jokingly said, "That's probably not the best idea." It's hard for me to put my thoughts into words in general. It's not something I was ever taught growing up, and so trying to put everything I felt and experienced after Asher's death into words on paper was even more of a challenge. But after going back and forth, she gave a pretty solid argument that the Lord (and many other people) had laid it on her heart that there needed to be a chapter in this book for dads. This chapter is simply what I personally experienced after losing a baby, written with the help of my wife and with the hope that other fathers can read it and possibly relate. My experience with the loss of our son, however, may not be the same as yours. I have learned that each person feels different things and grieves differently. But after talking with other dads who have gone through something similar, it seemed like many of us had similar thoughts and could relate to one another.

I grew up in a very large family. I am one of seven—the eldest boy but fourth in line overall. I have eleven aunts and uncles and over eighty-five first cousins, so family has always been important to me. I was always around so many young kids in our family growing up, always playing with them and helping to take care of them, so I have always loved the aspect of having young babies in my life.

So when we had our first two boys, Liam and Graham, I was so excited. As a new dad, there are things you've dreamt of doing with your children. And every part of the process—from finding out that your wife is expecting to hearing the heartbeat to finding out the gender and feeling the baby kick against your hand and then finally getting to hold them in your arms—creates joy in your life that you get to experience with this new person that God has specifically called you to raise.

You think about all the exciting and fun things you get to do with him or her, like teaching them to walk and how to ride a bike, throwing a football or baseball, going to dance recitals, helping them learn to read or practice their addition and subtraction, teaching them to drive, and the joy of telling them who Jesus is and that he came to bring us all to him in heaven. And then you think about who this new person was created to be. You think about what their personality is going to be like, what things in life they will love to do, and what career the Lord will call them to.

But there's also nervousness about having someone new that God has chosen you to raise, who you are now responsible for, and all of the realistic and responsible thoughts begin to set in. Things like the cost of all that comes with having a baby, including how you're going to pay for college and weddings, and the responsibility of raising him or her to be a God-honoring and God-fearing disciple of Christ.

When Rachel told me she was pregnant with Asher, those nervous thoughts set in more than they had during our other two pregnancies. At that time, I was going through a rocky time in my career, wondering if I was going to be released. I work in a very competitive job as a front-tire changer in NASCAR. It's a very demanding role in which very few mistakes are allowed. We have to perform at the top level and compete for our spots almost every week. At the time, NASCAR announced they were transitioning from a six-man pit crew to a five-man pit crew, meaning one of us was going to lose our job. And so, my main focus had to shift to ensure I could provide for my family. My prayers to God were to keep me focused on my job and to prevent anything that would distract me from doing what I needed to.

So when Rachel showed me that pregnancy test, I honestly was confused and upset. I tried not to upset Rachel with my response, but hearing that news just felt like one more task was added to my plate. And I hated that feeling because normally I would've been extremely excited that we were having another baby. But I honestly became angry with God, only thinking about how I was going to support another child if I didn't have a job. A few weeks went by where I continued to try to figure it out and do it on my own when, by God's grace, the Holy Spirit woke me up and softened my heart. He showed me that I was trying to do this all on my own and that I wasn't trusting in the Lord. He reminded me that God was going to take care of us—that he was the faithful one, not me—and reminded me of the times when he had taken care of me before.

He humbled me.

And I remember thinking, "Who was I to question God?" Sometimes as men, we feel like we have that right, to question. No matter who it is, or the consequence, we feel like we deserve an answer, especially when it comes to our family and the well-being of it. We skip over the thought that God, who created the heavens and the earth and everything in it, doesn't need our approval. He doesn't need to receive the OK in our lives because as our Creator and as our God, all things happen under his will.

The book of Job is such a great reminder of this. After Job experienced the loss of all ten of his children, his wealth, and all the thousands of livestock he owned, even though he was a righteous man that God called "blameless," he questioned God's ways, determined to make sure that God heard him: "Though he slay me, I will hope in him; yet I will argue my ways to his face" (Job 13:15 ESV). But God reminded Job of exactly who he was questioning in chapters 38 and 39. He reminded him of his power in creation, that he knows all and sees all, does the undoable, controls the stars and the skies, the weather and the light and the darkness, and that even the animals trust him to provide for and protect them. Sometimes we need that reminder too. I thanked God for that reminder of who he is and for settling my heart and mind, reminding me that my job is to trust in him, and I finally got to a place where I was so ready and excited for us to be a family of five.

I remembered what it was like bringing my first two boys into the world. It was such a surreal experience and taught me so much. Each of their births was very different. With Liam, they had to do an urgent C-section because his heart rate kept dropping and eventually wouldn't come back up. I was thankful I got to be in the operating room and was the first one to hold him. But there were moments when I was definitely scared, and my eyes were opened to the dangers that can come with bringing life into the world. Graham's birth, though, was completely different. I actually got to deliver him myself (with the doctor standing right next to me), which was one of the most amazing experiences of my life. And part of what the Lord did when he softened my heart was help me remember what God had taught me with my other two boys, and that made me eager to know what he was going to show me through Asher's birth.

The day came for our eighteen-week ultrasound for Asher, and we were both excited to find out whether this baby would be a boy or a girl. Since we have two boys, many people made bets on what this one would be. Somehow, I knew that it was going to be another boy, even though I desperately wanted a girl. After having two healthy pregnancies, though, we weren't prepared at all for what we were told in that appointment:

"I'm sorry. There is no heartbeat."

I honestly didn't believe it at first and thought there must have been some kind of mistake, like the ultrasound machine wasn't working right, and a million thoughts ran through my head. But once everything was confirmed, reality set in.

I expected the world to stop, but it didn't. It was hard for me to watch everyone else keep going about their day when our world had just stopped.

My first thoughts were about Rachel and all she was feeling and how I was going to help her. I then thought about our boys and how I was going to explain this to them. Our youngest was one at the time, and I knew he wouldn't be able to comprehend it all, but our eldest was three, and I knew there might be some confusion and questions. I then thought about my extended family and all their questions. I knew they would be wondering what happened considering we had two healthy pregnancies and babies. I knew eventually I was going to have to face it all, and it wasn't going to be easy.

Growing up, I was taught to forget my emotions quickly and didn't learn how to deal with them. And now I understand how much of an impact every person's upbringing has on their life. It impacts our marriages and how we understand what marriage should be like, it impacts our view of fatherhood and how we parent our children, and it impacts how we handle all that life throws at us. So as all this hit me, I had trouble knowing how to handle everything. The thoughts that ran through my head were, "Is it even OK for me to express emotion, or do I just need to push mine to the side and be strong for my wife?" I didn't know when the "right" time was to feel emotion or what emotion was right for a particular moment. And I desperately wanted things to just go back to the way they were. I wanted this not to be real and fought myself on trying to just push through it quickly.

I think one of the hardest things for me was not being able to fix this for Rachel. The pain was there from losing my son, but my brain was fixated on making sure that she was OK. I knew that my son's life was out of my control (his life and death were up to the Lord), and so I automatically focused on what I thought I could control—making things better for my wife. But I soon realized that I couldn't make this better for her, that her emotions were out of my control too, and I didn't know how to help her. I didn't know how to tell when I was making things worse or better or when I needed to be a shoulder to cry on. And even then, I didn't know if I would even be a good shoulder to cry on because I didn't think I'd be helpful. And this feeling of helplessness set in—my son was gone, and there was nothing I could do to help my wife.

I think a lot of men struggle with this. We as husbands have this innate drive within us to protect and help our wives and children and feel the need to put our emotions to the side so that we can help them in whatever way they need. One of the thoughts that ran through my head was, if I move through my feelings quickly, it will help her to be able to move through hers quickly too. Again, this is something I was taught, not to sit in my emotions or even feel them at all, and I assumed Rachel would think that way as well. Honestly, that drive within us to protect our wives and families is not a bad thing at all; it's part of the way God designed us, but sometimes it can get out of balance, and we don't take the time we need to untangle our own emotions.

My faith after losing Asher was really put to the test. I was very confused and upset with God because he had just helped soften my heart in trusting him with my job and having another child. I was so ready for all of it, so I didn't understand at all why he would allow this now. I asked him a lot of questions and didn't receive immediate answers. In fact, a few years went by before I felt like I was able to fully see the Lord's answers to my questions and the reason why he allows deaths and suffering into the lives of believers. But I understand now that the times in our lives when he makes us wait have purpose. I know that the Lord has us walk through thick muck and mud that make us feel stuck not knowing how we are going to make it to the other side so that we have no choice but to turn to him for help and learn to fully depend on him.

I don't have the answers to every question, but here is what I've learned and the advice that I would give to husbands and dads walking through the loss of a baby.

SURRENDER IN PRAYER

Come to me, all who labor and are heavy laden, and I will give you rest. Take my yoke upon you, and learn from me, for I am gentle and lowly in heart, and you will find rest for your souls. For my yoke is easy, and my burden is light.

—Matthew 11:28–29 ESV

After I understood that there were multiple things out of my control in all this, I was reminded that there is one thing that is always in my control: prayer. There are going to be days that will be confusing, frustrating, and painful, but bringing it all before the Lord is what will help. It's OK if you don't know what to pray for at first. Just begin by laying it all before him and asking the Spirit to give you the words you need.

Here are some things you can pray for, specifically, as the head of your household:

- *Pray for spiritual protection.* The enemy will be doing all he can to make this situation worse. Pray Ephesians 6:10–18 to arm and protect your family from the warfare that will be waged against them.
- *Pray for your wife.* Ask the Lord to bring her the comfort and peace that only he can provide, and ask him to show you how you can help her.
- *Pray for your children.* My boys were young when we lost Asher, but if your children are older, they will likely have a harder time understanding all this. Ask the Spirit to speak to their hearts and help them understand.
- *Pray for yourself.* Ask the Lord to give you that same comfort and peace, and ask him to help you untangle any emotions you might be experiencing.

BE PRESENT FOR YOUR WIFE

> Two are better than one, because they have a good reward for their toil. For if they fall, one will lift up his fellow. But woe to him who is alone when he falls and has not another to lift him up! Again, if two lie together, they keep warm, but how can one keep warm alone? And though a man might prevail against one who is alone, two will withstand him—a threefold cord is not quickly broken.
> —Ecclesiastes 4:9–12 ESV

God has given us the responsibility of caring for our families. In his perfect design, we are the heads of our households, and God is to be first in our lives, then our wives, then our children, then our jobs. Oftentimes, these things get out of order, so it's incredibly important to search your heart and ask yourself what is most important to you. Our responsibility as husbands is not just to provide for them and take care of them physically but to take care of them spiritually and emotionally as well. We as fathers don't have the same connection with babies as mothers do. That doesn't mean we don't have any connection, but it is very different. They feel all the changes that come with pregnancy, the pain of labor and then the physical pain of recovery, and they have much a stronger emotional connection with the baby. So this loss for them is a lot harder than anything we can imagine because we've never experienced it. Be patient with your wife as she processes this loss, and understand that it's likely going to take her much longer to heal.

It's tempting to distract yourself with life's tasks or work. It's easy to just start doing the next thing and begin moving forward. But your wife needs you to be present as she tries to process this. Helping her with things makes a huge difference, and small gestures go a long way. Listening to what she has to say and talking about it with her will help her be able to process all this. Sometimes her emotions or feelings might not make sense, but you don't have to solve the problem. I have learned that you don't have to have all the answers, but that just being there with her makes her feel safe and makes grieving a lot easier for her. Try to carve out a specific time each day to see if she wants or needs to talk about anything.

In marriage, God provides us with another person to help us and carry us in the hardest moments of life. What a gift that is. As you both navigate through this, lean on each other and help carry each other, but also understand that she will be leaning on you more, and you'll need to do more of the carrying as you both walk through this type of loss in your lives.

UNDERSTAND IT'S OK TO HAVE EMOTIONS

The Lord is near to all who call on him, to all who call on him in truth. He fulfills the desire of those who fear him, he also hears their cry and saves them.

—Psalm 145:18-19

Throughout Scripture, we see how God shows and shares his emotions—he is joyful, jealous, angry, grieved, and so on. And since we are created in his image and likeness, it is true for all of us that we all have emotions too. God created us to be able to feel emotions, so it's not wrong or weak to feel sorrow over the loss of things in our lives. It's true that we are not called to let our emotions rule us, but to completely disregard them is not what God intends for us. In fact, it ends up creating more chaos in our lives. The way we express our emotions as men, though, can look very different from the way women do. There is no right way to express emotion, so don't feel like your grief needs to look like your wife's or anyone else's. But when we can untangle and work through our own emotions, instead of just disregarding them, we are then in a place where we can effectively help others do the same.

LOOK FOR THE SPIRIT TO OPEN OPPORTUNITIES FOR CONVERSATIONS

> But in your hearts revere Christ as Lord. Always be prepared to give an answer to everyone who asks you to give the reason for the hope that you have.
> —1 Peter 3:15

Unfortunately, millions of families experience pregnancy loss. Which means there are a lot of other fathers going through the same thing you are. God created us to be in community with each other, and when we are willing to share our stories with others, we are able to be a part of bringing the kingdom of heaven to earth and helping those who are empty and broken discover the truth and love of Christ. Use this as your platform for sharing the gospel and bringing light into a dark world.

I'm sorry for the loss of your son or daughter. I know the pain, confusion, and anger you might be feeling and how all your hopes and dreams for that child are gone now. Despite all the pain and confusion, though, I am completely sure of one thing: God is good. Even in the absolute worst moments of our lives, he is good, and all things work together for his good (Rom. 8:28). The world is broken and full of people who are empty and hurting, but we get to change that. We have an answer to that brokenness and pain, but we have to make the choice of whether we are going to share that answer with the rest of the world or not.

Watching Rachel write this book with the Lord's help and take this tragedy in our lives and turn it into something that is going to help other people has completely confirmed what I knew about God beforehand but have now lived through. If I can help any other people through similar situations as I have experienced in life, then I am going to, and I encourage you to as well. Our purpose as believers is to shed light and encourage one another and work to build Christ's kingdom, keeping others from the clutches of the enemy. And this starts in your own household. We have been given an opportunity to share the light of Christ with others and to bring glory to God by allowing him to work through tragedy in our lives.

Acknowledgments

When I first felt the Lord calling me to write this book, I questioned him for months before I finally believed that his answer was "Yes." I couldn't wrap my mind around it. He was pulling me into something completely foreign. My degree was in nursing; I didn't have a clue about the world of writing and publishing. But none of that mattered. I got to experience the Lord working in me in a way that I never had. I got to watch him stretch and mold me in directions I would have never taken myself. And in the process, he taught me how to fully rely on him. To ride blindly and trust that when the Lord says that something will be done, it will be done, no matter the circumstances. And on this journey, he has given me everything that I've needed (and more), including gifting me with a village to make this book happen.

Austin. I remember the day I called you and told you I was going to write a book. You had just finished a race, and your first words back were, "Absolutely. I think you should." You had no doubts or questions at all, just complete confidence. Since that day, you haven't stopped encouraging me. Thank you for all the ways you stepped up to handle things at home so that I could do this—the many nights taking the boys to practices, handling dinner, helping with homework, getting lunches ready for the next day, taking them on weekend camping trips, or taking them out of the house for a few hours so that it was quiet for me. Thank you for pushing me when I needed pushing, listening when I needed to process, and comforting me through the biggest doubts and fears. And most of all, thank you for believing in me and always pointing me back to Christ. I love you and am so thankful I've had you by my side through every part of this.

To my boys, Liam and Graham. Thank you for the endless encouragement, all the soul-strengthening hugs and kisses, and the constant prayers every night before bed for God to "help Mom with her writing." You have been some of my biggest encouragers, cheering me on the whole way. I love you both to heaven and back.

Mom and Dad. As you raise your own children, you fully realize and acknowledge just how much your parents really taught you, and I was blessed with parents who took the time to teach me a lot. Thank you especially, though, for teaching me discipline, a strong work ethic, and the habits needed to complete a project this big. Thank you also for the constant encouragement. You know me so well and knew when my heart needed reassurance and prayer, and you offered it before I could even ask. Most of all, thank you for showing me how to prioritize my relationship with the Lord over anything else and leading me in my faith walk.

Tanya Pollard. I'm not quite sure I could thank you enough for the time you spent helping me with this book. You gave me more insight and wisdom than I could have ever dreamed. And your encouragement was *exactly* what my heart needed to hear every time you gave it. Most of all, you gave me the gift of a friend through the doubts, fears, and questioning. Thank you.

Nicki Koziarz. Oftentimes in leadership roles, it's hard to know the full impact you've made on everyone you've met and counseled. As someone whom you've impacted, I want to say thank you for everything. Your guidance, encouragement, and teaching have helped this author, brand new to the world of writing and publishing, in more ways than I can count. Thank you for sharing your wisdom, experience, time, and insights as my writing coach in the Book Proposal Boot Camp and for believing in the message of this book.

All my family and friends who helped watch the boys on days when I needed to get work done. Thank you. Especially my parents and my in-law family for the week-long stays, weekend camping trips, and cousin sleepovers while I worked. It truly takes a village, especially when you are raising children, to get a book into the world, and having your help with the boys was such a blessing.

Life Church family. You have surrounded us since the day we found out Asher was gone. Your prayers were constant, you gave the most thoughtful gifts, and for four weeks straight, we had meals provided every single night. And you have continued to surround and encourage us as this message was being written. Thank you.

The girls from the Book Proposal Boot Camp. Especially Britney Froese, thank you for all the encouragement, critique, suggestions, and guidance as I was putting together the bones of this book.

Leafwood Publishers. Thank you for believing in this message and the opportunity to partner together for this book.

References

How to Find a Christian (Both Individual and Marriage) Counselor Near You

When searching for a counselor, I urge you to seek out one that is a Christian, so that in receiving your guidance, you are being directed by the Word of God. Each of these websites offers a place where you can simply enter your zip code to find a Christian counselor nearest you:

- The Association of Biblical Counselors: https://christiancounseling.com/
- Christian Counseling and Education Foundation: https://www.ccef.org/counseling
- The American Association of Christian Counselors: https://aacc.net/
- National Association of Christian Counselors: https://nacconline.org/

Gift Guide

As awareness of pregnancy loss continues to become more prevalent, you can easily do a search online, be it on social media or Google, and find a company that creates and provides gifts for grieving mothers and fathers. Here are a few.

LAUREL BOX

Laurel Box is a company that offers curated boxes of personalized items for people who have experienced loss. You can either customize your own box with items of your choice, or you can choose from one of the boxes that are already put together. They have a multitude of gifts to choose from. Anything from custom ornaments and candles to handkerchiefs, jewelry, and seed packets. You can also specify the category, whether it be miscarriage, infertility, bereaved mothers, or something else.

   https://www.laurelbox.com

HOPE AGAIN COLLECTIVE

This company makes handmade earrings specifically for mothers who have walked through pregnancy or infant loss, and a percentage of every purchase is donated to loss moms to provide them with grief resources and help with medical expenses.

https://hopeagaincollective.com/

MYJULY27

MyJuly27 is a company that has created a beautifully unique shop for both mothers and fathers who have experienced loss. Uniquely, they offer jewelry and footprint canvases where they have approximated the size of footprints for each week of gestation, starting at week four and continuing through week twenty. They also offer name keepsake necklaces with specific diagnoses, such as anencephaly, intrauterine growth restriction, trisomy diagnoses, Turner syndrome, and more.

https://myjuly27.com/

COTTON STORIES

Cotton Stories is a company where the artist, Caroline, produces stunning sonogram and baby loss watercolor paintings. Mothers can send in their sonogram picture or a picture of their stillborn baby, and she can create a painting from it. This is such a wonderful option for mothers who have experienced early miscarriage, because oftentimes the only pictures they have of their babies are from an ultrasound. View her Instagram page, https://www.instagram.com/cotton.stories/, to see examples of her work.

https://www.cottonstories.se/

MOLLY BEARS

Molly Bears is a company that creates custom weighted teddy bears for families coping with any form of infant loss. You can send in the exact weight of your son or daughter, and they will create a bear weighing the same amount.

https://mollybears.org/